The Pathless Path

FINDING CLARITY, PURPOSE, AND INSPIRATION FOR THE NEXT CHAPTER OF LIFE

ERIC A. BLASER

Capucia LLC
211 Pauline Drive #513
York, PA 17402
www.capuciapublishing.com
Send questions to: support@capuciapublishing.com

Paperback ISBN: 979-8-9920502-1-9
eBook ISBN: 979-8-9920502-2-6
Library of Congress Control Number: 2024927252

Cover Design: Ranilo Cabo
Layout: Ranilo Cabo
Author Photo: Michele Gruenwald
Editor and Proofreader: Jennifer Crosswhite
Book Midwife: Karen Everitt

Printed in the United States of America

Capucia LLC is proud to be a part of the Tree Neutral' program. Tree Neutral offsets the number of trees consumed in the production and printing of this book by taking proactive steps such as planting trees in direct proportion to the number of trees used to print books. To learn more about Tree Neutral, please visit treeneutral.com.

Praise for *The Pathless Path*

"If you are ready for a life that is truly your own—unconventional, grounded in freedom, and designed moment to moment—this book is for you. (And if you're not yet ready, read this anyway and get yourself ready!) Life on your own terms truly is possible, and *The Pathless Path* can guide you there. Eric Blaser has spent his life gathering this wisdom and shares it—raw, real, and right on time. Seize this book as a journey to your very own soul...where all the answers you seek await."

—Dr. Kymn Harvin
International Bestselling Author
*The Soul of America Speaks: Wisdom for
Healing and Moving Forward*

"The most remarkable thing about Eric's book is how it starts as his story and then evolves seamlessly to become everybody's story...if one is willing to do the required work of deep introspection that leads to openness and, finally, change."

—Arthur Redillas
Former university Admissions Director
Current navigator of mid-life change

"In his latest insightful book, Eric Blaser reveals how he broke free from nearly three decades of emotional sloth and stumbled upon a new life plan that actually works, offering a roadmap to fulfillment, success, and genuine happiness. Want to join him on *The Pathless Path* and figure out who you are and where you're going? Here is the answer."

—Terry J. LaBrue, BA, MA, APR, author of *Literary Feast*

"Life is full of challenging transitions that aren't easy to navigate. In *The Pathless Path*, Eric describes, with insight and humor, how he has taken the important space and time alone to be present in his life and to discern what *is* from what *was*, to find his way forward. He offers exercises to help us discern our own circumstances more clearly, to move step by step toward a life that fulfills our spirits as we act on the possibilities of the gifts we each hold. An inspiring story and helpmate for pathfinding in a rapidly changing world."
—Wendy A. McClure, community builder, facilitator

*This book is for everyone embarking on the journey
of self-discovery.*

Two roads diverged in a yellow wood,
And sorry I could not travel both
And be one traveler, long I stood
And looked down one as far as I could
To where it bent in the undergrowth;

Then took the other, as just as fair,
And having perhaps the better claim,
Because it was grassy and wanted wear;
Though as for that the passing there
Had worn them really about the same,

And both that morning equally lay
In leaves no step had trodden black.
Oh, I kept the first for another day!
Yet knowing how way leads to way,
I doubted if I should ever come back.

I shall be telling this with a sigh
Somewhere ages and ages hence:
Two roads diverged in a wood, and I—
I took the one less traveled by,
And that has made all the difference.

—Robert Frost
"The Road Not Taken" (Frost [1915] 2015)

CONTENTS

Creating a Life That Works for You

Midlife, like any large life transition, can be an unsettling time. Something inexplicably changes. Not only do you become aware that the years are passing, but you begin to wonder what is really in your heart. Are you still on the right path? You may feel a deep need to explore yourself and understand what all the discontent is about.

On the surface, you may have a good job, a house, a comfortable social status, but something feels off. You're longing for something but can't put your finger on it. What's going on?

You might try talking to friends and family, but they say you have it so good! There's nothing wrong. Stop thinking so much or just be grateful for what you have.

So, what do you do? How do you reconcile this growing discomfort?

Midlife is often the time where we must give ourselves a chance to reevaluate the people we've become. Over time, plowing ahead, doing tasks and activities that were expected of us, we might have ignored our inner nature. We haven't nurtured ourselves or reflected upon who we are. Our outer lives might have changed and grown, but our internal operating systems might have become outdated.

This is what happened to me.

Congratulations for picking this book up. You're about to go on an adventure of *your* life. This book is about a journey that, once embarked upon, will cause situations and events to open up in your life like well-orchestrated plot shifts in your favorite movie. You won't see what's coming, but circumstances will unravel so beautifully. For you to *make* that happen, you'd need Oprah's entourage to pull it off. But to *let* it happen, you just need courage. This is what I call the Pathless Path.

The Pathless Path person is courageous enough to look for a new way unique to them. You could be wanting to be an entrepreneur, an artist, or to be self-employed. You may feel stifled and bored working nine-to-five or for other people. You may feel called from inside to be more, even if you don't know what that means. But you are afraid to go forward with your dreams or ideas because you can't see either the dream or the way very clearly. This book can illuminate the journey.

But first you have to understand where you are. Like a GPS, you can't orient yourself until you start moving. As the new information begins to come in, you might feel resistance and doubt. We get afraid to try something new. So we decline and endure where we are.

The Pathless Path is a journey taken one step at a time. As soon as your mind gets involved, the doors of innovation close, because your mind thinks it knows what it is and drastically reduces your possibilities.

It's our mind's job is to keep us safe. Our ancient ancestors were hardwired that way. The mind says, don't step out of line, don't leave the tribe, you'll be rejected or end up exposed and be eaten by lions.

Nowadays, it's our peers or family who might reject us, or we who might reject ourselves, judging by our past failures. Our lack of self-love can keep us tied to what we know and prevent us from moving forward.

What is required is just our willingness to explore and be curious about a life we care about. Pathless Path people know what they want but not how to get there. They're open, receptive, and can see all sides to a subject. They look for win-win situations. They are playful and present and maintain a state of joy from the endless things in life to be grateful for.

This book is designed in three parts. The first part describes the Pathless Path. How do you influence existence and let it work for you? The second part is about connecting and grounding to your roots. Your personality, your nature, skills, values, knowing and clarifying yourself. The third part will help ground you in the present so that you can see the story of your life and the obvious next direction and can avoid pitfalls.

Throughout the chapters, there are suggested exercises. They are included to help you better understand yourself. Try them out if they feel right. Try on being curious about yourself even if you think you know already. See what happens.

Throughout the book, you'll read about my experience discovering the Pathless Path during my midlife crisis. It started when I paid up-front for a summer-long cabin stay on an island in the Puget Sound, without even the security of a contract. I didn't have a job or know anyone. I was completely out of my comfort zone. But it felt right, and the island felt like home.

At first, I had an agenda. I knew how my sabbatical was going to go. After my stay, I planned to go home and go onto the next thing.

But nothing went as planned. After a struggle of will, I surrendered and went into darkness.

Once I did that, life opened up in ways I couldn't imagine. It was like Joseph Campbell says; I stepped into a life that was waiting for me. Everything flowed easily. I wasn't expecting to get a job, but one came. I began to get more perspective on my life. I uncovered an undiagnosed learning disability, and more things began to make sense. I wrote in seventeen journals and took over 10,000 pictures on the island. I read and thought and followed what inspired me and what felt good.

During this time, some organizing force supported me. Money kept appearing. I was challenged in ways beyond anything I thought I could endure. It was scary at times but also exciting. I wanted to be inspired before embarking on the second half of my life. I began to learn from my own journey.

And for my whole life there was this whisper of authorship. I didn't know what it meant. But after years of exploration, I began to understand why the voice kept calling.

What Is the Pathless Path?

Most people are living fixed and predictable lives. They "know" things. But this "knowing" is usually fixed. It kills our ability to access the energy of imagination and creation that allows us to develop beyond what we know.

Creatives, artists, innovators, adventurers, and entrepreneurs are likely on this path. They value freedom, adventure, and creativity. They might have an idea, a vision of what they want, but they don't know how to get there. They are Pathfinders: Those who are courageous enough to find a way unique to them.

To be on the Pathless Path means having a general idea of where you want to go, but instead of making something happen, you wait for inspiration. You take one step at a time. Any more than that means your mind/ego is taking over and is trying to keep you safe by knowing and planning. The Pathless Path is steeped in trust that everything will somehow work out. If you trust yourself, take responsibility for your actions and your lot in life, have faith, and follow your inspiration, you'll get to where you want to go.

The Pathless Path is unique to you, your environment, circumstances, and people around you. It is hard to see, but you get glimpses. It is like a flash of lightning illuminating your way. Pathless Path people don't get caught up with the lightning; they look at the path. The inspired action they choose is based on what occurs to them along the way.

For example, you might have a simple desire to travel. You can imagine places you'd like to go. You can see yourself taking a plane, train, Uber, etc. in a different country. Then you come across a brochure about Japan. It strikes you, and you imagine being in Japan. It feels good! On your way to work, you meet a Japanese exchange student who is struggling, not sure which train to take. And you're holding the brochure for Japan, with a picture of his hometown. He smiles, and you exchange numbers.

This is it. A new life can show up for you with this kind of synchronicity. Charles Eisenstein said synchronicity is an orchestration of life that comes through a deeper intelligence, into our body and heart (Eisenstein, 2021).

Now we do need some certainty and a general idea what to expect in our environments and to have some general goals, but it's important to manage a balance, keep some mystery, and allow some space for the divine to join in. Otherwise, we are going to look for distractions to spice up our lives, like addictions and infidelity.

Metaphorically speaking, the Pathless Path is like a new song I discover and I really like. I experience it. It moves me. It awakens feelings within me over time. But knowing it too well can kill it.

On the other hand, if I listen to a song with words I can't understand, it stays interesting even though I've heard it hundreds of times. I ask myself, why? Then I realize that because I can't understand the words, the music resists knowing. I cannot consume it. Because of this, I can experience the music again and again, like new.

The same thing happens in our lives. If we respond to what we see and hear, without trying to know or explain it, we can cocreate with the universe. We just have to be present and be surprised by what shows up. On the other hand, our jobs and partners can become like a stale song. Our knowing can make them redundant and boring. Because we already know what they're going to say or we expect the same behaviors over and over, we ourselves help make that predictability, even though the other person might be trying to change.

You could change this by deciding to ask yourself, who are these people today? What's different about my job now? You could also practice leaving space for them to respond differently or respond differently yourself, then look for subtle changes. The experience can refresh and reinvigorate your life.

Now, you might be wondering, "How do I get on this unmarked path?" The Pathless Path is like going to sleep at night. You know that if you want to sleep, you slow down, turn down the lights, lie down, close your eyes, and maybe take a deep breath and release the tension in your muscles.

But sleep is something you can't make happen. It happens to you. It's done for you. It's grace. You do all the things you *can* do to invite it, and then you have to surrender. Try to go to sleep. Try being the doer of your sleep. The very act of trying keeps you awake.

The same is true with the Pathless Path. This is what I mean when I say that knowing interferes with it. But, like inviting sleep, there are some things you can do to create a conducive environment so its grace can bless you.

Stories are one way of creating this environment. Stories have a way of conveying things beyond the literal words. Our oldest metaphors are known as myths. They're not supposed to be taken literally. They are conveying truth of another kind. But stories about real-life events can convey truth and meaning too. Let me give you an example.

During the end of the pandemic, I decided to take a trip down to Southern California. I needed a change of culture and food and a reprieve from the isolation of living in the woods on an island.

While in Desert Hot Springs, I walked up to a palm oasis. At midday, the temperature was already in the low nineties, warm for early November. In my childhood, I'd read a book about an oasis, and since then, I'd always wanted to see one. Water in the desert always sounded exciting. As I closed in on a grove of seventy-five-feet-plus native palm trees, I could see water flowing at the base of them.

The San Andreas fault had ripped the earth's crust here and exposed the aquifer. The contrast of the dry rocky desert and tall palm trees inspired me. I felt a flood of creativity, and I sat and wrote in my journal. The feeling lasted into the next few days until my departure.

Returning the rental car in Burbank required a lift. The airport was only ten minutes away. Instead of taking a taxi or an Uber, I was inspired to ask someone at the rental place if they could give me a lift. What did I have to lose (open, playful, adventurous)? They said someone could, if I didn't mind waiting. I thought, *why not?* I was still grateful for my trip and in new adventure mode.

Soon I was in a van. A young kid was driving. I smiled and said, "Wow, you're young!" stating the obvious.

He said, "Yeah, I just got out of high school."

"I'm old," I said, wrinkling the skin on the back of my hand. I asked him what he liked to do.

Without skipping a beat, he said he liked to edit his friends' skateboard videos. He said he did it for free. But he was also in a management program with the rental agency. He said, "If I finish the program, they will pay for school. Then I can manage my own store in three years."

I asked him to imagine five years down the path, if he stayed with the management track at the agency. "How do you feel?

Hmm... as he drives, missing the turn.

By now I was feeling like Yoda and he was Luke Skywalker here. I had no idea where this conversation would take us, but I was just being curious and present and listening.

He answered, "I think it would be good. My family hasn't had much opportunity."

I said, "Now imagine five years from now editing videos you said you liked." As I said that, we were driving past major Burbank studios. "How would you feel in five years from now?"

He smiled and let out a sigh. "Yeah."

I continued, "The videos are a path that's not clear. But I'm here to tell you, even though you can't see the video path, if you start out on it, roads will open up where there seem to be dead ends. But first you have to go down that path for the doors to open."

"Ah I see," he said. "That makes sense." The energy was ramping up.

I said, "The choice is always yours."

He went on, "But I have to hurry and figure it out."

I said, "No you don't. The path will open up whichever direction you take. You can't make a wrong move." It felt like a beautiful moment. I said, "You can do videos on the side if you like. You live in the film capital of the world. Now you have experiences in the two paths. You choose."

Feeling blessed, I felt inspired to say, "Thank you for the opportunity to have this conversation."

He said, "Yes, thank *you*!"

After my encounter with the young man, I had to ask myself, after delving in midlife for almost six years, how would I express the differences between a midlife crisis and how it felt to be a young person struggling to figure out what to do? Both might be looking at an unfamiliar path. Both might be trying to decide whether to choose the safe and comfortable one or to follow a passion.

The Younger Person	Midlife Adult
Hurrying to start career	Reevaluation of career
Afraid of the unknown	Needing to explore
Unknown versus safe	Old life versus redirect
Practical versus passionate	Boredom versus authentic
Outward focused	Reconnect with self
Pressured to please others	Pleasing self

The Younger Person (cont.)	**Midlife Adult (cont.)**
Crisis to belong	Experiencing existential crisis
Feeling obliged	Reconnecting authentic self
Conforming to social norms	Dropping out of social and organizational rules

This is when I realized I would like to help people take the Pathless Path. I thought of everything we typically tell young people, all the college prep schools preparing us to work in factories or retail or as providers of services. I wanted to hold up a different light for people to see. Like the Hermit card in the tarot deck. In the Ryder Waite tarot deck, the Hermit is holding up a lantern. Some regard it as a symbol of taking time to contemplate life issues.

The next chapters in part one are not about how to get onto the Pathless Path but about what it feels like to be on that path already. It's about feeling the urge to do nonconforming work as an artist or innovator or entrepreneur. What the life is like. There are exercises in the coming chapters to give the *sense* of it.

It may be scary for you to trust being yourself authentically. Will I make it? Will I be supported financially? Will people still like me? What about my family and friends?

A lot might change! The Pathless Path will get you there. Trust one step at a time, set loose goals, and most of all, trust that all will be well. Learn to be uncomfortable with the unknown, respect and love yourself, and take responsibility for the journey you're on. It's your life.

Here is a poem I wrote about becoming, trusting the process, and allowing your own nature to come through.

A Farmer Plants Corn

They know the process the seed needs to go through to become corn.

He knows he's not going to wake up and find corncobs in his field the next day.

It's a process of becoming…

What does the corn know?

I cannot sit in this shell forever. I must break out of here.

If it's in the right environment, the seed swells and cracks its hard prison of its known world despite its fear. It realizes, I'm using up my reserves in here.

So, it puts a feeler down to find out what's out there in the earth.

Down it plunges. If it is lucky, the environment will be good, finding moisture and nutrients beneficial for growth. What were those strange markings inside on my shell walls?

Then, God willing, it sticks its little green head out of its shell and orientates itself to the light.

Deeper its roots go, grounding into the earth, and it stretches further up toward the light. The seed may not know what it is becoming, but it feels right, and its nature is to expand.

It may get glimpses of tassels and long silky hair so unlike its undulating leaves. It might wonder, is this all there is to my life, unfurling yet another long leaf?

What is this great itch emanating from my sides? Where are my new leaves?

Wait, I think I'm dying. What are those sprouts coming from my sides? Am I losing my leaves?

Ah.... I think this was what was inscribed in my shell...

Grow and reach your potential. Trust the process. Let it unfold. Reach high up into the sky.

Bear fruit so others can remember too.

Won't you join me and say yes to that voice?

PART 1

FEEL THE PULL

Soul Calling

CHAPTER 1

Your Own Relativity
More or Less...

I'd told very few people back in Portland, Oregon my plans. Now, the crowds of July Fourth tourists snarling up the Washington State Ferry system were gone. I had just arrived on a remote island, not knowing anyone.

I climbed up a wooded ridge along the Puget Sound and was looking over at an apple tree clinging to the crumbling cliff's edge. What the hell was that doing here? Somehow, it was exactly what I was feeling about myself. My guess was not many people ventured up here, but the plentiful deer certainly had.

I was relieved to be here finally, sitting on the edge of a cliff, watching a fishing boat head out toward the straits. For the first time in many years, I watched the clouds float by.

I had plans to resurrect an old screenplay, learn the violin, and be the captain of my boat. But most of all, I wanted to figure out what was next, and eventually find a life that worked for me.

Dictionary.com (2020) describes relativity as "dependence of a mental state or process upon the nature of the human mind": Relativity of values, relativity of knowledge. By relativity, I mean that each of us has unique life experiences that have shaped our values and given us a perspective different from anyone else's. Because of our differing experiences, some things definitely feel right or wrong to us. But other things feel neither right nor wrong. They feel, rather, like something we might want *more* of or *less* of.

Granted, our schools and our general exposure to a similar culture prepare us for a collective life of understanding and consensus. This helps to unify us, but unless we also get in touch with our own personal values and experience, we are living out someone else's perspective: our family, caretakers, teachers, or others.

If we listen to our own inner guidance, we can find clues to what is good for us. If you asked me how I knew a job was for me, I might close my eyes for a second and think, *how does it feel?* Is the prospect stifling or exciting? Does it make me feel peaceful or energized?

Accessing your sense of relativity is different from using your reason. I'm not talking here about pros and cons. I'm saying, does it feel good? Or feel heavy and burdensome? This is how to use your relativity. You and only you know if something is right for you.

How do you know whether to say yes or no to an invitation from a friend? The conventional way might be to ask them more about it.

Who will be there? Where will it be? What will be the ultimate benefit? Will you connect or network with someone there? All these aspects are possible.

Or, you could close your eyes for a second and feel if this is right for you. Does it feel good? Or feel heavy and burdensome to go to the party? In this second approach, you are using your own relativity. Only you know if it's right. You may not be aware of how you usually determine whether an event is right to go to, because your process has become automatic. You might not be used to testing your relativity.

Now try applying this to your desire for change. Perhaps your job or current career is no longer satisfying. You need a change but don't know what to do. Without a clear direction, it might be best to follow your relativity. When applying this to your job now, you could say, is this serving me? Does it feel right? Or what aspects of it do you like and want more of, or less? What inspires you? Is it time to move on?

My original attempt to understand my relativity was back in 2015.

I loved plants; I'd been in horticulture my whole life. I started early, cutting down all my neighbors' shrubs at age five. I was mowing lawns at sixteen and worked my way through college at a plant care company. After working in nursery establishments around Portland, I started my own business.

I never had to advertise. For many years, I enjoyed being a personal garden coach helping clients create and envision their garden, as well as doing small jobs and artistic pruning. In 2013, I took a new job as an estimator for a tree company while holding onto my best gardening clients. After twenty-five years, I wanted to see if I could work for someone else. I was excited to learn more about the language of trees. Trees are like people. Their age, environment, and species, along with certain life events, determined what I was looking at with a client.

I liked educating these clients in a holistic way and having them choose the course they thought was best. But this took time and lots of energy and was in direct conflict with the company's ideas. I wanted to educate myself and my clients. The company wanted me to tell them what they needed and to be efficient.

600-square-foot atrium

My home brought me great joy. In the middle of Portland, I had created a tropical oasis inside a tall, 600-square-foot atrium. I also had had three other greenhouses. Sometimes I potted up plants late into the evening. Once, my neighbor saw me and said, "Don't you ever stop work?"

I said to him, "I'm not working!"

He looked at me with two thumbs-up. I felt this way for a long time. My life was good. I'd developed friendships with my clients. It was a great joy. I thought it was going to be my life forever.

Then, something began to happen. I remember the daily drabness of life passing like a certain numbness. I put out the yard debris can weekly, but it felt like every other day. I felt no connection to my life. It was just a blur, like I was doing time. I couldn't understand it. When did things turn? I hadn't seen it coming.

I happened upon a documentary called *Finding Joe* (Solomon 2011). The documentary was based on the work of Joseph Campbell, the author of the famous book, *The Hero's Journey.* It talked about arriving at the point of our lives where we hear a call for adventure from within. My soul cried out.

I must have watched it thirty times, and each time, I cried. This was a powerful message to me. I had to discover what was going on inside.

I wanted a life that worked for me. A life that fit me. I wanted a life that suited my true nature and personality, that aligned with my values, my skills, and life experience. I wanted to look beneath into my internal conflicts, beyond what I already knew about who I was and who others thought I was. I wanted to know what I wanted and what was safe and where I fit.

I tried to make these questions into goals to focus on, but it was difficult. The harder I tried, the more difficult I found it to focus. There had to be a way to find a life that fit me!

In hopes of reigniting my passion for horticulture, I bought myself a ticket to the Chelsea Flower Show in England as a fifty-first birthday present.

I knew most garden books were about "garden rooms," and I enjoyed helping my landscape clients create a sense of connected spaces around their homes. But something urged me to think more about the transitional spaces. What features could I use to draw people forward and into the next space? What is the space in between? I wanted to explore the threshold of change, liminal spaces in gardens.

In England, there were arches, steps, containers, and strategically placed plants, which drew your attention. Sometimes, long narrow corridors of hedges funneled you into an opening of the garden room, just like a river would in nature. The idea of these features was to excite people's curiosity, and therefore inspire them to keep moving and exploring.

I was intrigued by the liminal spaces, but not as excited as I expected to be about new plants or garden rooms.

Back in Portland, on my familiar walk at my favorite public park, Crystal Springs Rhododendron Garden, I thought about the trip.

Crystal Springs Rhododendron Garden Portland, Oregon.

Why hadn't it inspired me as others had in the past? I had been to botanical gardens all over the US and British Columbia, but none were as impressive as the Chelsea Flower Show. What was wrong with me?

I felt exhausted. I had to do something. My heart wasn't into it anymore. I began to realize I was going to have to expand beyond what the past had taught me. I didn't know what to do. I felt change coming.

I had read about divine discontent, how we always want something more than what we have. But this seemed different. By now I was familiar with the concept of relativity.

I paused on the bridge over the cold, clear water and decided to try it out. I watched the ducks paddle on the pond and the golfers swatting balls in the distance.

So what was my relativity? What did I want more of in my life? Or less?

I was living alone with my cat, Edwene. I loved having all the space to myself, and if I left a mess, it impacted nobody. I had trouble with romantic relationships, and I was comfortable living alone with lots of freedom.

But maybe I just needed to tweak things a little. Maybe I needed a little more of something.

In early February, a friend of mine knew someone who needed housing. I offered him my extra room. It was a long time since I'd had a roommate, and I liked the idea. It fit the "more of" category and seemed to be the right thing to do. Housing was tough to find in "Sofa City."

I enjoyed living with him. I got to share ideas, food, and music. But after the newness of a roommate wore off, my discontent returned even bigger. Portland, this destination spot, was feeling empty to me.

Hmm. What now? By then I'd done some kind of work in almost every neighborhood. In the years since the '90s, the city had become unrecognizably crowded. Trees I loved had disappeared in construction projects. A drive across the city used to take twenty minutes. Now it could take two hours.

I knew that if I asked anybody, they'd tell me to stay. I didn't really know what to do, but I had to go in some direction!

I surrendered. Then I remembered a story someone had told me.

It was a woman I'd met at a casual onetime career class, eight years before. Suddenly, I remembered her describing a kayaking trip she'd taken in the San Juan Islands. I'd been mesmerized by her description of paddling alongside orcas, watching them breathe and play. She'd described the small seaside town of Friday Harbor.

Somehow this story was vivid in my mind. It wasn't logical, but it felt like an opening.

I told my friend about it, and a few weeks later, in September 2015, we left to spend a long weekend in Friday Harbor. I was willing to explore and compare it to Portland.

On the boat from Anacortes to San Juan Island, my relativity was off the charts. As the boat hummed across the sea, I could feel this tremendous tidal pull of something. Where was this coming from? There were hundreds of islands around me. Which one was calling?

We arrived in Friday Harbor and were soon out on the water. I'd forgotten how much I missed kayaking. Our trip coincided with the full moon, and the tides were extreme. There was a huge upwelling of columns of water and whirlpools. The currents were strong as a river but in salt water. I had never seen anything like this.

I felt a great sense of peace as I paddled on the water, but the guides were bug-eyed. The strong currents concerned them. At times, I thought I was going to be carried away by them. They often yelled for us to keep up. I was just so curious about the sea. I looked down on the kelp forests. The tall plants leaned from the current. They looked like trees with their floating tops and long braids of brown leaves. We didn't see any orcas, but I wanted more of this place.

I heard the call to explore, and I was ignited. Even though I didn't know exactly what this was about, I felt a definite switch from "see what happens" to "I have to go back."

Perhaps you, too, know the feeling of old ruts holding you in. Perhaps you, too, know the moment when you break out. The Pathless Path gives you one step at a time. What's calling in your life? Where are you pulled to? Have you crossed over to *must*?

Test the Urges

On the drive back to Portland, I could feel this sense of dread and numbness descending on me. This confirmed for me I wanted change! I knew I had to return to the San Juans again.

I began to do some research. I met a former Portland gardening client who warned me about the difficulty of making a living out in the islands. She said it takes time to get established. You have to take a few different jobs to make it. The cost of living and the lack of housing was a problem.

But she loved her community, the nature, and the relative calm and peace she found there. Another friend on one of the islands said if he lost his housing, he'd likely have to leave. I understood the challenges, but I was determined to find the source of the calling.

The second time, New Year's weekend 2015, was dreadfully cold and foggy. It was barely above freezing. As I tried exploring an area of Whidbey Island, I hit fog and ice, spun my truck on a curve, and landed in a ditch. I was a bit shaken and surprised I was unscathed. My truck was fine, too, except for the sword ferns and sod stuck in the bumper. I left them intact for character.

Whidbey Island, though, didn't seem right. I had a few extra days because of the holiday, so I thought I'd go to Victoria, Canada.

Maybe that was the origin of the pull? Because the purpose of my trip had been to follow my relativity, I hadn't made specific plans.

After studying the ferry schedules, I realized the ferries would eat up all of my remaining time. Now what? I looked at the San Juan ferry schedule.

I now recognize this experience as provoking the divine and allowing the Pathless Path to inspire a direction. Something was out there, and I was determined to find it. At a loss of where to go, I randomly picked Lopez Island.

Lopez Island Ferry Landing.

The ferry ride was obscured in fog. I wondered how the boat could navigate. It felt like a metaphor for my life. This was crazy! I couldn't tell anyone I was wandering the San Juans looking for some sign. It made no sense in a world where we are expected to have some "conscious" idea of what we are doing.

"Lopez Island!" The ship's loudspeaker woke me out of my thoughts. The landing, still shrouded in fog, remained mysterious. I drove off the ferry, up the hill, and started to have an overwhelming sense of home. It was similar to what I'd felt in Portland twenty-eight years ago. In those days, people said, "You're moving where? Why?"

I drove warily by feel on unknown roads in dense fog, remembering my earlier crash, but still, I felt an overwhelming sense of familiarity. What was this? What did it mean? Was this what had been calling?

I found a road on the south end of the island that looked inviting. The trees soaked up some of the fog, and I could get a faint glimpse. I parked and walked along the road and found a deer path that led me to a cliff's edge. A bright spot emerged in the sky. Briefly, the fog lifted.

I saw an unobstructed view of the Olympic Mountains with the sun shimmering off the sea. I stilled and felt the warmth and sheer beauty of this spectacular view. Once again, I felt the presence of nature and its endless possibilities and its reflection in my life.

From this distance, my job at the tree company seemed even more stressful. Driving in

Olympic Mountains after fog lifted.

traffic, managing client expectations, following up on issues, dealing with work crews, and my frightening weekly sales quota. My remaining gardening clients, once a source of fun and creativity, were exhausting too. I didn't know why I'd grown tired of answering gardening and plant questions.

Try It Out

I'd experienced a clear sense of home and felt an opening for more.

But was I just blaming Portland for why my life wasn't working? Lopez was a stark contrast to Portland, yes. But was it really time to move on and change?

After all, I didn't know anything about Lopez Island. I knew I had to test the urges, put myself in this place, and explore this relativity. I had to examine what this feeling of home meant. What else would I like more of?

Only you know if it is time to leave your job or move to a new location.

For myself, I had hundreds of questions.

Second time out to the island. Ship with tug sparkling like diamonds.

The next time I visited Lopez, it was February. I watched the ferry part the sea and watched the islands pass. A few small boats and a freighter looked like a mother duck and her ducklings. The water shimmered like diamonds in the sun. It was refreshing to be traveling and watching the scenery. I felt a great relief and anticipation about what I was going to discover. This time it was sunny!

Lopez still had that feeling of home. I could see farms and the small quaint center of habitation called the village. I found the school and the library and stopped at one of the coffee shops in town. I sat and listened to the conversations of the locals. Later, heading south, I saw sheep, cattle, and a lot of open hayfields. I stopped at the South End Store to read the community board. I just followed my instincts. What was it like here? And why this feeling?

For the next five months, I returned once a month, testing my feelings and trying it out. I asked myself, what am I needing in my life?

First, I wanted to try living in a small town. I wondered what that would feel like. I saw hints that I might be more of a small-town person. I'd often visited Sauvie Island, about thirty minutes northwest of Portland. I had dreamed of living there.

Second, I wanted to be closer to nature. Not just visiting but living in it.

And last, I knew I was over driving. I resented the traffic, congestion, and the wasted time in a vehicle. On the other hand, I loved having thirty minutes in my car while I let the ferry transport me!

One evening, I found myself having dinner overlooking Fisherman's Bay. A few remaining winter boats glowed in a bright yellow-orange sunset. I sat there for a long time, sifting through the feelings I was experiencing. I felt connected to life again.

The third time, I camped out. The great horned owls hooted all night. At one point, the full moon peeked through the clouds and illuminated my tent. I stepped out and watched the billowy clouds pass. I felt rooted to life again. Somehow, being here was awakening something inside me. I felt this familiarity. This wasn't some onetime euphoric event. There was some consistency now. I liked being here, and it felt good. Something was here for me.

Where in your life have you had similar feelings? What's missing, which if you had it, might make you feel more content and connected?

One thing I knew was that whenever I needed some clarification in my life, going into the woods or a garden always revealed some answer. Just the act of observing nature could get me out of my logical thinking patterns and into a more receptive state, where the small still voice could surface. Somehow, the walking and movement in nature returns me to myself and restores me, opens me to answers, to foreshadowing events, even clairvoyance.

On the other hand, actively looking for answers seemed to separate me from existence. It's like my mind saying, "I know better." It disconnects me. Rather than being an active participant with life and with nature, my mind is telling me, "Leave me alone. I got this."

But the truth is we can't look for truth. It just reveals itself. We can recognize it. How does it feel?

I was beginning to understand that my feelings were real and to trust them. In the past, I'd had difficulty acting and following through with what I felt.

Now it seemed like, after living in a city for twenty-eight years, wanting to move wasn't running from anything! Still, it wasn't logical. Logic was saying, "Are you stupid? You're not twenty-four anymore. Bounce back from this? You don't have any cushion!" Financially, I was still recovering from the great recession.

Remember, the Pathless Path is often illogical.

Suddenly, I dreaded the thought of living life without a safety net. It made me sick to my stomach. My logic didn't offer any answers about what I was experiencing and gave me no sense of whether Lopez was the right place.

But walking in the moonlight and hearing the owls seemed like a sign. First, I'd have to be clever. And second, even though I didn't have answers, the path would be illuminated.

Back in Portland, nobody knew what was going on with me except for an older gentleman named Phil. He was also known as Pathfinder Agate Man. He had a house with roommates and welcomed wayfarer travelers. He was seventy-nine when I met him. As a former English teacher, he knew myth and story as a part of man. I occasionally saw former students walk up to him in gratitude for the difference he'd made in their lives.

He was cultured, educated, and adventurous. He listened to me without judgment, and he understood what I was going through. Without his willingness to listen and to guide, this midlife crisis/soul calling would have been much harder. He was an important elder in my life.

Again, I found myself walking through Crystal Springs Rhododendron Garden. It is fed by hundreds of springs, which push up throughout the garden and fill a pond next to the golf course. The water is cold, still, and clear, perfect for reflecting the rhododendrons and fir trees.

On this walk, it occurred to me to ask for a six-month leave of absence from the tree company. Okay, if Lopez didn't work out, I could at least figure out what was next! What did I have to lose? I might lose some of my customers. But it was worth asking. One step at a time.

The truth was that I was scared to death. For at least two months, I delayed asking. It wasn't until my coworker confided to me that he was in the running for a position as city tree inspector that a fire was built under me. I thought, *Great, now if he leaves, I'll lose my chance*. I had to make the request while I still could.

In the office above the manager's desk was a calendar I'd made for her from some garden photos I'd taken in England. She pointed it out and said she loved it. I didn't often talk to her, so I felt awkward as we exchanged a few pleasantries. At last, I blurted out that I wanted a leave of absence.

"Is that why you went to England?"

"Yes," I replied. "I needed a reset, but it didn't help. I just need some time to think about things."

"Sure," she replied. The break meant I had to give up my phone, car, insurance, and retirement during that time.

Now, I had a new set of worries. Where the hell was I going to live on Lopez? There was already very little housing, and summer was coming.

I put an ad on the local community pages and didn't hear anything. I called Realtors, and nobody returned my calls. During every visit, I checked the local postings for something. Nothing! It was the end of May. My leave started on July 1. It was coming down to the wire. Now what?

Meanwhile, my roommates wanted to take over my house, plants, and cat while I was gone. They got a third roommate, and I turned the care over to a management company I knew.

Joseph Campbell describes hearing a call from inside for something greater in your life. And if you embark on that journey, "Doors will open where there were walls" (Solomon 2011).

I had no reason to believe this was true. I just knew that whether I had a place or not, I had to go. I had to take responsibility for my life, even though I didn't have all the answers.

If you were to try to figure out everything in advance, it would be too complicated. Even if you did one of those flow charts with options, you couldn't do it. Which option should I take? From here or there? What now? Every decision leads to another possibility. Like a branch of a tree, the further out you go, the more possibilities there are. This is why I suggest you follow your relativity.

Chapter 1 Exercises

More or less

Take an 8"x11" or larger piece of paper. Draw a circle. Divide it in half. Label one as More and the other as Less. Here you can practice relativity in your own life.

a) Close your eyes and take three deep breaths. Put your feet on the floor, and sit up straight. The purpose here is to be open and receive your own guidance from the greater self that resides in you. It is there waiting for your return.

b) Imagine a cord of white light extending from your spine to the center of the earth. This is your grounding, your foundation. Feel the connection to the earth, which sustains all life, including you.

c) Open your eyes.

d) Let the ideas and thoughts come. You don't have to be orderly here. Enter them in either one column or another. Try to alternate columns as an experiment. See how your body responds. Are you contracting or expanding? Are you filling in one column more than the other?

e) If you're having difficulty in the More category, think of what you were interested in as a child. Maybe this is still relevant to you today.

Try it out

Is there anything that stands out in the More category? Is there something that calls to you to be more expressed? For example, let's take painting. If you thought, more painting, then:

a) Try painting three times a week for an hour. You may space them out as Monday, Wednesday, and Friday, as an example. Once may not be helpful. You're trying relativity here. How do you feel during the painting? Do you want to paint more or less?

b) The Less category could be challenging as well. For example, you might have a friendship that's not fulfilling to you, and either you need to ask for more out of it, or it needs to end. Is it one of those relationships that could fade away, or do you need to explain why?

c) With your eyes closed, practice thinking about your current job. How do you feel? What are you missing and want more of? Pay attention to your senses. Now imagine if the opposite is occurring. What would that look like? How do you feel? Did you sense a shift? Can you swing between the ideal situation versus the current situation? What is that like for you?

CHAPTER 2

Opening to Possibilities

How Do You Know You're Alive?

In the first chapter you learned to recognize your soul calling: Those things you needed more or less of in your life. You tested the experiences by investigating further. You tried some new things out. Now it's time to open up to the greater possibilities those answers and experiments implied.

This need for adventure is not easily understood by the logical mind, let alone by your friends or family. But now you have arrived at a metaphorical lake to cross, and you don't know how to do it.

Not knowing is a great place to begin. At this place, everything is available to you. As soon as you let your logical mind say, "I got this," you can exclude other opportunities that might exist beyond your known reality. It's important to know that when you choose what direction to go in, you're telling existence, "I got this." However, if you choose yet remain open to other possibilities, you are still allowing yourself access to untapped potential.

If you're uncertain, simply hold the need to cross the lake. How will you do it? I don't know. Necessity is the mother of invention, they say. Yes, I do want to cross the lake: goal.

Allowing yourself not to know sounds like what religions call faith. But the kind of faith I'm talking about doesn't require you to have religious beliefs. It just requires you to remain open to the universe of possibilities you aren't yet aware of. Yet to someone who is used to basing their decisions on rational thought, going forth not knowing might feel almost suicidal. And for people with ADD who have difficulty focusing, even the idea of a goal can seem horrible. For those people, the act of mental attention is, for the lack of a better word, offline.

It has taken most of my life to understand and accept my diagnosis of attention deficit disorder (ADD). When I was in school, no one knew about it. I only knew that, for me, the harder I tried to focus on doing something, the harder it was to do, so I avoided doing anything that needed attention. I procrastinated and then failed. Then I compared myself with others and judged myself. Over the years (and I'm sure some of you can relate), I told myself (and heard from others), "Just focus!" I asked myself, "Why can't I get it together?" And "What's wrong with me?" I looked at others who could focus and get things done and wondered, "Why can't I?" And the results were devastating.

These judgements created a deep-seated shame. I thought of myself as defective and I overcompensated by overworking, doing too many things. I hid my lack of self-esteem beneath the stress of being overworked and the difficulty of being overwhelmed by too many things. These excuses made me feel normal but left me socially withdrawn. I wondered why I couldn't be like my peers.

Still, people often commented that I had interesting things to say or that they saw me as unique, someone who heard my own and different beat.

During my sabbatical, I decided boldly to create a life that worked for me. It would be my way, not anyone else's. I wouldn't try to fit in but rather try to look for the gift in my ADD and how it helped me to see the world differently.

But after my sabbatical began and the exhaustion began to fade, those familiar feelings of doubt and shame crept back in.

Finally, I had to face my worst fear. *Maybe I really am crazy*, I thought. Maybe I have a serious mental issue.

I sought out a psychiatrist to ask. And I was willing to accept that yes, maybe so…?

At the end of the session, he said, "There's nothing wrong with you."

What a relief! Once I began to accept that this is just how my brain worked, I started to look closer at how this difference affected how I saw and went through life. When I did this, I recognized something I'd taken for granted: I avoided thinking by experiencing.

In my effort to avoid focusing, I'd been able to remain more open. I was always on the edge of being and doing. This lack of focus let me see and feel more widely than many other people and allowed more passion and creativity. Not relying on logic or goal setting allowed a different kind of intimacy with the tasks I did.

Michael Meade, modern storyteller and author of many books, including *Fate and Destiny* (2010) says that where there is difficulty, right next to it there is a gift. He says, each of us is born with limitations, but those limitations are also gifts.

So how could having ADD be a gift? How did it affect the way I saw the world? What I understood from the psychiatrist was that my mental bypassing (avoidance of focus and goal setting) had allowed me to develop other forms of intelligence. My therapist said it was common for people with ADD to go forward not knowing.

Meanwhile, back at the lake. Instead of figuring out logically how to cross it, focus on the other side of the lake, and open your intention to pure possibility. Open up your heart in anticipation of an experience. You don't know how, but it will be done.

Let the unseen forces—life, breath, myth, and mystery—collide and engage the muse, the vortex, matrix, existence, or whatever you want to call it.

On my soul's journey to Lopez, miraculous things happened. I couldn't have logically figured out how to accomplish many of them. The point was just to find the courage and go anyway.

By courage, I don't mean fearlessness. Courage means feeling the fear and doing it anyway. Courage is what allows us to grow by giving us the experience of life supporting us, even though we let go of what normally keeps us safe.

In contrast, staying focused only on being safe in the world of familiar constructs, logic, science, planning could be killing you inside. Sticking with any old job because of a sense of duty, acknowledgement, and confirmation, even though that job doesn't let you use your true talents and gifts, could leave you spiritually crying for more. To compensate for this, you might be accumulating material things to fill that hole.

Once you start on such a journey, it's easy for others to judge you and think you are being irresponsible. They might accuse you of not wanting to work, not wanting to contribute to society. "Just get a job! I did!" People might accuse you of bailing out, being a coward, being reckless.

There are exceptions to what I say, but the point is that this journey, if taken with caution, small step by small step, always checking to see whether you are in alignment with your goal, is neither cowardly nor reckless; it is heroic.

Figuring everything out takes the mystery out of life; it cuts us off from the mythical stories that enrich our lives and guide our souls and breathe meaning into purpose. Relying on logic can make us passive or fatalistic. Why climb the mountain when I can see it on TV?

Because it's not the destination that matters, it is the experience of the journey you've embarked on. These new experiences of places and people will change your life. You'll confront yourself in uncomfortable, unfamiliar events that routine life cannot expose you to. You'll touch your purpose, metaphorically speaking.

It's who you'll become as you cross that lake and who you'll be on the other side that matters.

At a virtual International Society of Arboriculture conference in 2021, I heard the opening speaker cite this quote from Viktor Frankl. She said, "Between stimulus and response is a space. In the space is our power to choose our response, and in our response lies our growth and our freedom."

Now, let's do a little groundwork. First, you can be open. This just means being receptive. Say yes to life without adding anything else. Leave anticipation, expectations, and judgements behind. Show up empty! Let the way reveal itself.

I call this space a clearing. Don't plan on what you're going to say. Just be present with a person or event, whether it's a coworker, spouse, friend, grocery clerk, or foe. Let go of prior patterns or judgements. Just be open to the possibilities. By doing this, you may notice something never before seen in a friend, or you may notice a change in a coworker because you didn't fill it up with what you already know.

An example of letting life unfold is when I tried returning store merchandise without a required receipt. I wasn't trying to *get* something; I didn't know if I'd get my money back. I just approached the situation to see what would happen. I showed up *open* to all the possibilities.

The important thing was not what I wanted; it was who I was being.

When I approached the situation with this attitude, the clerk smiled and exclaimed, "I hate receipts too. Hold on." She went and got the manager, and my return was approved.

If I'd driven to the store while anticipating what would occur, plotting my strategy, rehearsing what I was going to say to the clerk, I'd have missed the experience of driving and of being in the present moment. Instead, I let that be a mystery, an adventure. I showed up delighted, then let it unfold.

Again, in my life, this is how things unfold. I rely on a ferry system to get me to the mainland. I get up, prepare, and do all the things I need to get in line and get to my appointments and errands. There are no reservations. There are quota limits for each sailing but no way to predict how many cars will be in line. I never know if I'm really going to get on. I show up, and I leave it up to the ferry gods to decide what adventure will unfold today. A breakdown, a pod of orcas, a crew delay, a crisis, or a smooth ride. Who knows? I've done my part. I'm at peace, and most importantly, I cannot be disappointed.

Having friends can be a journey. Holding on to what you've already experienced with them helps to hold them in the old pattern. By being present with others and leaving them room to change, you allow growth. Similarly, leaving room in a romantic relationship can allow something different to show up, something that might breathe more life into it.

I encourage you to be an empty plate. Relax, breathe. This helps you become present and alert. Let the situations and events in your life be a collaboration of unfolding.

If being mindful is new to you, it won't be consistent at first. A driver is only as good as his last trip; a chef is only as good as their last dish. But this is okay. It's a moment-to-moment experience. To be human is to be imperfect. You're learning. Be easy on yourself.

I practiced this in my life for a number of years. It has changed me but not in the way I expected. Something miraculous happened. I'll leave you with this. To paraphrase Joseph Campbell: People aren't looking for the meaning of life; they're looking for the experience of being alive (Moyers 2011).

Your Life Is Waiting for You

Moving closer to the direction of your longing will bring you closer to what Campbell calls "The life that is waiting for you."

My joy is seeing people shaking off those obligations, those ideals that might make us look competent, smart, and successful on the surface but make us feel soulless and empty inside.

Have you ever encountered a public servant who's grumpy? I recently went to the DMV to renew my driver's license and gave my address as a post office box. The woman who took my application looked at it and glared at me. Then, in a deep, froggy voice like something out of *The Exorcist*, she said, "You don't live in a mailbox!"

Her annoyance bothered me. On my way home, I pondered what had provoked such a response. I decided she was either having a really bad day or she was living for the future. She was doing this work, waiting for retirement so she could do what she liked. Meanwhile, she was spewing her unhappiness out on the public. Now, that is playing safe with a huge cost.

But even if we know what our unhappiness is costing us, how do we know if the change we choose is going to be right? What if it turns out to be a big mistake?

Russel Barsh of Kwiáht, a local conservation educational group here on Lopez, presented a talk about the Coast Salish First People who inhabited the San Juan Islands before white settlers. He says that these First People allowed those in their tribe to do what they felt inspired to do. It didn't matter if you were a male attracted to basket weaving or a woman who wanted to hunt. They left each member of the community free to decide what they wanted to do, based on their own inspiration. In modern times, we somehow got this all messed up.

These days, without the encouragement and safety of a tribe, stepping out into the unknown takes courage. Sometimes we don't do it on purpose. If you are not in the right line of work, and not doing what is yours to do, you can get hit with the proverbial cosmic 2x4. It could put you in position to get fired, have a health crisis, get into an accident, experience a divorce, and so on.

These things happen to us so we can discover who we are at a deeper level. Michael Meade refers to this as the death of the little self.

This death requires us to reach down and touch our inner resources so we can be rebirthed to a larger idea of who we are.

Whether you've embarked on your journey willingly or unwillingly, you may find yourself standing by the abyss of the unknown.

When I paused my job at the tree company, I had no idea how much change I was going to go through.

Author Elle Luna in her book, *The Crossroads of Should and Must: Find and Follow Your Passion*, (2015) writes:

> It is here, standing at the crossroads of should or must, that we feel the enormous reality of our fears, and this is the moment when many of us decide against following our intuition, turning away from that place where nothing is guaranteed, nothing is known and everything is possible.

Robert McKee, the renowned teacher of screenwriting, describes the trials each hero has to go through in coming to know themselves. In a movie, if we see the hero sipping coffee alone in a café, how do we know who he is? We only know who he is when he's being challenged. Only then, will the choices he makes reveal his character and his potential.

These events happen to us so we can be stronger and reinvent who we thought ourselves to be. Whether we choose this journey into the unknown or it chooses us, we instinctively try to grab onto what we think will keep us safe. At the time, it is difficult to remember that the process of continuing on this life adventure will change you into someone you had no idea you were capable of being. That it will give you an opportunity to connect with something greater than the day-to-day life so familiar to you.

FEAR

(Osho) Bhagwan Shree Rajneesh

It is said that before entering the sea
a river trembles with fear.
She looks back at the path she has traveled,
from the peaks of the mountains,
the long winding road crossing forests and villages.
And in front of her,
she sees an ocean so vast,
that to enter
there seems nothing more than to disappear forever.
But there is no other way.
The river cannot go back.
Nobody can go back.
To go back is impossible in existence.
The river needs to take the risk
of entering the ocean
because only then will fear disappear,
because that's where the river will know
it's not about disappearing into the ocean,
but of becoming the ocean.
(Rajneesh 1987)

What are you becoming?

The Power Behind the Little Self

Even if we agree to open up to the possibilities around us, to take some risks and even make some mistakes, what if we go too far? What if we end up changing not just our lives but our*selves*?

Carl Jung suggests a child's persona is created when the mother has to leave them at some point to do her own work. Because she can't be with them all the time, they need to create their own identity. This ego, or "little self" grows, and we come to think this is who we really are. But below this is the larger self, our true nature. It is grounded in a connection with nature and with our love for others. It has infinite knowledge and potential for understanding.

Most of us go through life believing we are the smaller self. We identify with our ego. But the larger self is always behind the scenes. It reveals itself in experiences I'm sure we have all had. The phone rings or we get a text, and somehow, we know who it is before we answer. Or we come to an intersection with a green light, yet we hesitate, only to have a car run a red light on their side. How did we know?

I've talked about the cosmic 2x4 that can happen when you're on the wrong path, but there are times even when we're feeling happy and fulfilled, when our lives get upended. We call them black swan events. We lose our job, a loved one dies, we experience a natural disaster. We didn't see these things coming. We didn't choose them. The death of what was throws us into a new situation.

These are uncomfortable losses, even tragedies. But they're also opportunities to know ourselves at a deeper level.

Whether we entered a period of disruption because we needed more or because we lost what we had, we're going to feel fear and anxiety. Who we are is no longer. The ego's identification no longer exists. This is normal.

This is a passage we have to go through if we are to become a new version of ourselves. We have to change the way we view ourselves. In essence, we die to what was and go forward to the person we're becoming.

Osho, a spiritual teacher and author of many books, says we die but there is always more. Usually, we are losing a smaller version of ourselves and birthing a greater identity. We experience these events of letting go all through our lives. Each time we do this, we experience a change in our internal navigation system, or as I like to call it, our Innernet.

When this small identity runs on autopilot, it knows, judges, compares, and is right. It sees things in terms of us-versus-them. It gets hurt and offended by people and things. But there is more to us. This bigger presence is inside and waiting for your acknowledgement and attention. You've likely experienced this growth and guidance already, without being aware of it.

An example would be graduating from college and getting a job. Now, instead of gaining knowledge in the classroom, we are applying it to the real world of work. So, we're going to have to behave differently. If we continue to act like students, we might get fired. We have to leave behind those parts that no longer serve us in the new environment and develop new ones.

When we experience a midlife shift, what and who we were is no longer. We have to adjust to not only what we're now doing but how we now see ourselves. We might need help to see and make that transition. If we try to explain it to someone with no experience of life changes and transformation, it can make us feel isolated. This transformation is sacred to you. Sometimes it helps to find a coach, mentor, or teacher who can understand its essence and significance.

Sometimes, people show up to guide us in places we don't expect. I've mentioned Phil. We met when we were both part of a team for a mutual friend who was passing. He seemed to be a wise elder and counselor in that community. As I felt the growing urge for more in my life, we became closer, and things began to get clearer for me.

I remember one particular event. After seeing the movie, *Wild*, starring Reese Witherspoon, I had the urge to go to the Bridge of the Gods, which spans the Columbia River between Oregon and Washington. I had no idea why. Phil drove me there on a stormy day. He stayed in the car, and I went alone. After paying my fifty cents to cross the bridge and walking to the span, the wind seemed to increase. I thought I'd better run instead.

What I didn't anticipate as I neared the span was that the asphalt ended. In front of me was a metal grate. Which made it appear I was jumping off a cliff into the wind-whipped river hundreds of feet below. Terror ripped me. This little voice said, *"Keep going."* I crossed a liminal space. The horizontal rain was now stinging my face. The howl of the wind in the girders further increased the stakes. I had to trust I'd be okay and not blown off. A greater life was born on that bridge.

Later, in the comfort of a restaurant within the view of the bridge, I described the experience to Phil. He smiled. I felt invigorated. The adventure seemed to make me feel more alive.

"Do you see the symbolism?" he asked.

"Yes, clearly there is something more for me." On that bridge, I'd felt something new stirring inside. Something that wanted out.

Phil in a cafe overlooking The Bridge of the Gods, Cascade Locks, Oregon.

Spending time alone is essential to the process of letting go. It is important to find time free of distractions, so that you can become aware of this greater knowing as it emerges. Spending time in nature, observing plants and wildlife, is a good way to be quiet and listen for the source within.

Joseph Campbell talks about connecting to the power/presence of your larger self; he calls it "following your bliss" (Campbell 1973). We enter the doorway toward the divine by being a vehicle through which that divinity can be expressed. And one way through that door is to follow your bliss. Everyone can do this. And I can say everyone has experienced some bliss.

Chapter 2 Exercises

Experiencing

Pick a routine event you do daily, weekly, or monthly. It could even be your job.

a) Put aside all past experiences and expectations of what you already know about this familiar activity. For example, who you're expecting to meet, how the event will go, how long it will be, and what you're going to say or do. See what happens. Is there something you haven't noticed before?

b) Take a different route to work. Who cares if it takes longer to get there? Leave some time so you can stop if you're inspired to. You're on an adventure. Notice the things that interest you and watch what draws your attention. How do you feel, going to work this way?

c) Pick someone you regularly talk to or interact with. It could be the checker at the grocery store, a teller at the bank, or someone at work. Practice being present and empty in that interaction. Yes, you want groceries, or you have a job to do. But what comes up if you pay more attention to the person than to your objective? Do they respond differently to you?

Stay as present as possible. Leave an opening like a clearing for possibility. You don't know what is going to happen. Anything is possible. Pay attention to their expression and what comes up for you in the interaction. Listen to how you feel inspired to respond.

Longings

This exercise is just to daydream.

a) Go back and think over your life. Touch on things that come to you. What are those feelings associated with? Go back to days in your childhood that draw you there. Are there things you have forgotten about that want to be expressed? What comes up for you?

b) Think about something you'd really like to do but don't know how. For example, surfing. It has to be a real and true desire for this to work. Hold the thought and desire in your mind. Write down on a piece of paper *surfing* somewhere where you'll see it. See what comes up in the next day/week/month related to it. Be open for guidance from unsuspected places.

Life behind the little self: touching sky

a) Create a bold vision for your life. What would you like to see? At this point, don't worry about money or time or any other obligations. You have all the skills needed. How would you spend your time?

You get to be daring; don't worry what people would think. What do you feel inspired to do?

The clearer you are, the more you will be able to warp the universe. Your boldness and clarity aligns thoughts, desires, and feelings. As though you are guided by unseen hands, you may accidentally bump into the very person you need to help you turn your desire into reality.

If you're not clear, that's okay. Perhaps you've had many years of denying your wants and needs. Now is a time to change. You can explore yourself in further chapters.

b) Have your friend or trusted partner read you this one.

Hold out your hands, palms up, bent at the elbows, eyes closed. In one hand are your current experiences of who are, what you do, and where you live. Feel it in your body.

In the second hand, hold your bold vision for yourself. What do you want to create? Feel that in your body as well. Guess what? You're in the middle. And now you have permission to change.

PART 2

CLARIFYING WHO YOU ARE

CHAPTER 3

Who Are You?

Journaling

During transitions, going back to your roots and rediscovering who you are as well as listening to who you're becoming, can be an important part of your next chapter. There are a lot of tools at your disposal. Journaling is the first of these. If you find it difficult to write, you may be more comfortable keeping an audio or video log.

Journaling can be a gateway of discovery, if you are not sure what career direction you want to go in. You can converse with yourself, and over time, cues and desires can repeat themselves and you can see themes developing. The important thing that many will tell you is to be honest with yourself.

You can write what you'd like in your journal. It's yours. If you find you're getting excited about a certain idea, play with it. If you're thinking "I can't do that!" then, it has likely come from the right place. Trust your body and your instincts.

Remember, our minds tend to keep our desires small and safe. Try it out for yourself. Play with it. What does it feel like? Did it come from your heart or your head? Whose voice are you writing in? A teacher's, a parent's, or your own?

Journaling also helps to process emotions, unresolved issues, and conflicts with others and yourself. Over time, you can develop your inner voice more, and it will help with your guidance.

Two weeks before I was supposed to leave for the island, I still had no idea where I was going to live. Then I got an email from a couple who had a cabin on the south end of the island. It was a one-bedroom and close to the boat dock. I was relieved. Housing finally. My only concern was they didn't want a contract, and I'd have to pay cash. At this point, I had to turn off my city mind. No contract? And, I'd be giving these people $3,000.

My gut didn't give me warning signals. I decided to stick with my new resolve, to go with the flow, and figure it out.

During the last few weeks at the tree company, we were going to prune a tree, but there was a boat parked underneath it. The guy was going to have to move it. He said he wanted to sell it. It was a 14.5-foot 1965 Sea Swirl motorboat. Just the craft for the inland sea of Puget Sound.

I wanted it. I dreamed of being the captain of my own boat. The money I paid him for the boat, he used to pay for the tree work. I love exchanges like that. Win-win. Another customer needed some street trees planted, and I did that in exchange for a fiddle and some lessons. Again, I just wanted to start doing new things!

Finally, on the week after July 4, off I went, with two friends driving the U-Haul truck and my Toyota truck pulling the boat.

I was planning on boating, practicing the fiddle, and finishing an old screenplay. I was excited! I felt this relief. For now, all was good. I made it to Lopez and got settled.

The cabin was tucked away off a dirt road with ample room for the boat. It had wood and electric heat. The landlords were great. I'd lucked out.

On my first day alone, I sat on that bluff near the apple tree for hours. I lay and watched the clouds go by. Some slowly spun and expanded while others seemed to vaporize into thin air. I felt like a kid again. I was so relaxed and at ease.

I journaled for a while and just let the words flow.

For the first week I just rested. I went to the boat dock and walked along the beach.

Apple tree on bluff overlooking a harbor.

A week later, I launched the boat. The clip holding the line to the gas tank split and came off. I was stuck out in the harbor and had to paddle back. Thank goodness the former owner was meticulous and had left a paddle in the boat!

Still, I wasn't so sure about this boat business. I realized how little I knew about being a captain, and suddenly it seemed beyond what I wanted to know or grow into. I hated it. So much for this idea, I'd rather be watching the scenery go by or looking for sea life than looking out for rocks and other boats. It had been great in my imagination, but the reality was too much! Thank God I hadn't run into trouble out in the straits in strong currents.

The local transfer station had a place called Take It or Leave It (TIOLI). If I'd known this was here, I would have left the U-Haul in Oregon. TIOLI offered everything imaginable: bedding, clothes, small appliances, furniture, kitchenware, and so on. People with vacation rentals or second homes would clean everything out and bring it there for free to keep it out of the waste stream. Anything a person would take to Goodwill or just throw away was there, for free.

After getting over my initial exhaustion then getting my place set up, I began to feel a growing sense of isolation. I started to crave connection. I found on my visits to TIOLI a real chance to talk with people. Otherwise, I was alone in the woods all day.

I also realized I was going downhill fast! After six weeks of resting, I was really out of shape, both physically and mentally. I was used to gardening and landscaping almost every day. I might have been in a rut, but I had been fit and engaged in life. Now, I wasn't engaged at all. My utopian dream of doing nothing evaporated as I realized the whole midlife crisis might have been to the reaction to my exhaustion.

My fantasy of retirement burst. I began to realize, in this time of rest I'd so desperately needed, that it was essential to be engaged in life, or otherwise I'd waste away. And this time represented a passage into the next phase of my unfolding life.

I realized I'd been a person who likes to work at what I love. My problem wasn't that I didn't want to work. And I now knew I wanted to stay engaged in life.

But what's supposed to happen next? On one hand, I wanted to start filling my life with something new, and on the other hand, I felt like I was avoiding something that had been clawing from deep within.

I started my screenplay again, but it was met with resistance. Something inside was telling me no. I didn't know what that meant. I had always dreamed of completing it.

Now, resting from years of almost nonstop work, I could feel my anxiety rising. I had a sense of unfinished business. I had loved gardening, but the thought of going back made me feel tired. My heart wasn't into it. I was conflicted.

I realized I had this anxious need to fill the space in my life with something. My head wanted to jump in and figure out what that was, while my heart knew I needed to continue the sabbatical. Somehow, I needed to be in this limbo space and give my heart a chance to be heard. Otherwise, I might be going once more from the frying pan into the fire.

I wanted to explore myself, these conflicts I was feeling, and create a life that worked for me. I decided that instead of running impulsively into the next chapter of my life because I was afraid of not knowing, I would stay in the in-between, the liminal space, and give myself some time to process both my past and my feelings about who I am now.

I decided to trust life, and that if I didn't decide what to do, things would come my way that would be better than what I could have imagined.

One of these things was a book, *The Artist's Way* (Cameron [1992] 2002). She recommends that we just begin to write regularly, and that if we do, things will start happening. I knew I wanted more creative expression in my life, so I decided to commit to journaling every day.

On an excursion to Bellingham, I stopped at a bookstore for a new journal. For whatever reason, the brand of journal I liked cost three times more here than Oregon. I don't like ordering online, and I wasn't going to Oregon. I'd tried other journals and didn't like them. Clearly this was a money thing.

I meandered the store, frustrated. I knew what I wanted; why didn't I get it? Just because it was cheaper somewhere else? I laughed at myself and went back.

Now, another woman was standing there with a friend, discussing which journal to get. I smiled at the coincidence and talked about my dilemma. I said this one worked for me, but I was being cheap, and I'm back to get the one I liked. It's mine. My practice.

We laughed, and she chose the one she preferred.

I developed a routine that nurtured me. It was awkward at first. My first activity was meditation. I went for a long walk in the woods and came back and journaled. I would write about things that mattered to me. I was doing this for me and no one else.

While writing, I remembered an important lesson I'd learned from a mentor. He called it learning how to learn. This now came in handy for journaling in isolation. He said when an issue arose that bothered me, to go into it instead of avoiding it. Feel the feelings. Where do they originate? What event happened in my life that this current event or circumstances was pointing to? Was this old story still serving me?

I began to notice that if something bothered me about another person, it was usually due to a judgement I had about an incident. Sometimes there were parts of me that were lost or stolen or that I had forgotten about. Sometimes there was something I didn't like about myself, and I saw it in another person. Psychologists call this projection. It is something we all do when there's a part of ourselves we don't like. We can feel disgusted when we see the same thing in another person.

I initially assumed that working to exhaustion was the cause of my angst and conflict and the need for change. On a deeper level, I sensed it as a repulsion toward and resentment of horticulture. As with many emotions, this one wasn't logical.

Now I began to notice that deeper emotional issues had been hiding in the dark. They'd been buried by all the years' busyness. But, they had a life of their own. Now they were starting to surface.

I began to trace my choice of work back to its origins. I have often said I had gotten into horticulture work by accident. I didn't choose it. It chose me! Now I began to see this wasn't exactly true. When I was growing up, my home life had been chaotic. I couldn't find patterns that made sense to me, and plants offered an escape from the confusion.

Plants don't lie. They don't hate you one day and like you the next. Plants are benign. They just are. With good care and understanding, they respond by giving back in the form of flowers, lush leaves, and energy. Plants either wilt when they need water or are waterlogged with rotting roots. The difference was easy to figure out.

On the other hand, people would say one thing and do another. My mother would criticize me for being selfish when I was simply looking out for my own needs. If I didn't, she'd accuse me of being helpless.

Early in my life, I got praise and recognition for growing great plants. I loved doing yard work at home and for neighbors and worked my way through college caring for plants. After getting my BBA in management and human resources, I'd arrived in Portland, Oregon, and applied for entry-level positions requiring my degree.

As it happened, those jobs had all been taken up by an influx of Californians with much more experience than I had. So out of necessity, I'd fallen back onto what I knew I was good at. I felt connected to plants, and they brought me joy. I enjoyed learning about them too.

For years, I'd been in bliss, growing and propagating plants for myself and my clients. Gardening soothed my ADD, and I could focus better. It worked until something changed. Almost without noticing it, I began to resent all my plants that needed care.

When I'd realized this, I'd about died. I had been wet with sweat and tears. If I lost horticulture, who would I be?

Now, seeing myself from a distance, I felt dramatically changed. I felt an immense energy release. I felt born again. This was just the tip of the iceberg.

In another journal session, I wrote about the acknowledgement of passing the age of fifty. Back in Portland, watching my friends and clients age always reminded me of my own mortality. I felt like I had this bank account of years. Each birthday felt like going to withdraw some money and seeing the balance dwindling. How do I want to spend the rest of my life? Where? What circumstances? These things I wrote about.

But the people I was meeting on the island were new. I couldn't tell if they had aged. It gave me a new sense of safety. I felt ageless, like Superman or Dracula. Now I just wanted to try new things, even if I ended up changing my mind. I wanted to see new places and meet new people. My life felt more like an unfolding adventure.

My journaling helped me to connect to my life's meaning and to get closer to my new purpose.

Meanwhile, I'd never felt so isolated in my life. I was an introvert by nature and tended to isolate, but this was too much. I had to do something. I knew without a doubt that I was in the right place. It felt good to be here. I had always wanted to live in a small town and be a part of the community. But how would I meet people here?

I made a sincere effort to ask existence for help. I meditated about it. *Please help me with this feeling of isolation.*

The next day, I had this urge to go to TIOLI. I didn't know why. On earlier visits, the gal working there had been trying to get me to volunteer. I always said I wasn't ready. But this time, she said that there was a temporary paid summer position available. Really? I didn't even think about it. I just knew it was right.

I started the position as a traffic controller on the weekend. For five hours a day, I managed the fast-paced summer traffic of tourists and locals. For most of my life, I had taken most things personally. I thought I was mostly the cause of other people's behavior. But after a few weekends, I started to notice that if I said the same thing to everyone, being kind and helpful but still trying to keep the traffic flowing, the public was the public. Everyone reacted differently. Some people joked and played around; others were angry at me. For the first time, I could see that people's reactions had nothing to do with me. It gave me this sense of freedom. I wasn't responsible for how everyone felt.

I began to play with what I said to people. I felt liberated. Something about this position was going to teach me a lot about this new person I was becoming. I liked this place! And this work was going to be important.

Where in your life are you conflicted? What have you forgotten about? What's missing in your life?

Meditation

If you are confused and looking for clarity, one way to sort things out is to meditate. Over time, if you observe yourself like a movie, you can begin to understand what are thoughts, what are feelings, and who is watching this whole damn drama? And then maybe inspired things can emerge from seemingly nowhere.

Instead of feeling trapped by events as they happen directly to me, meditating allowed me to become the observer, the actor playing the part rather than being the director trying to control events and circumstances, trying to fix the drama on hand.

This isn't easy, and yes, I still get caught up in the drama at times, but I have become much better at recognizing it. It might seem paradoxical to think that by going inward, we are going outward. But knowing where you are lets you see things more clearly. You might ask, how do I get outside of myself? How do I know that meditation will help?

I'd learned the importance of meditation by going to the Unity Church in Portland. One of the ministers swore by it. She said she never started a day without it.

What activity would be so great that you would do it every day? I had grown tired of losing myself in work and doing everything for other people. I'd focus so much on the task at hand, I would forget about what I needed and where I still had to go. I left myself out of the equation. At the end of the day, I'd find myself arriving home in my truck, sitting in the driveway in the dark, cold, hungry, and still needing to unload my tools. And I had to cook. Who was taking care of my needs? What the hell was I doing this for?

The truth is, I was a workaholic. Work helped me feel normal, and the movement soothed the ADD. Growing up in the chaos at home, I hadn't had the validation I'd needed to give myself a better start in life. It had left me with a limited sense of self and made me socially anxious. Work helped me hide this.

But I couldn't keep doing this. If I put myself first, before my clients, could it improve my life? If I wasn't doing great, how could I serve my clients? Wasn't I worth this? I'd started meditating every morning, creating time and space for myself.

When I started doing this, I was really exhausted. Therefore, it was very easy to sit still. An East Indian teacher named Osho taught a Kundalini meditation. It involved active fire breathing (rapid guttural breath), movement, catharsis (emotional release), and then quietness. When it was time for quiet sitting, it was easy. So if you have trouble sitting for meditation, just get some good physical exercise.

With meditation, I began to pay attention to the thoughts and beliefs I held as they came up. By just watching and asking questions, I'd gained some self-knowledge. Whose voices was I hearing? My mother's, a teacher's, sibling's, or was it me? I paid attention to my feelings. Did they arise from thoughts I held, or did my feelings come first and then generate the thoughts? This all goes back to the idea of learning how to learn.

For example, if I was sad, I could ask myself, "Hmm, where did you come from? Were you sad first, and then were you thinking you were a failure?" Just watch these things that come into your screen.

Over time, I began to really enjoy my morning meditations. I looked forward more and more, as meditation helped me become much more present and see the bigger picture of my life.

I realized I'd already developed a meditative quality from horticulture work. Working with plants had given me the experience of focusing on me, my actions, and the task at hand. As I cared for gardens, the right action came into my awareness without any conscious planning or thought. Over time, I watched how the plants responded to my care, and using this sense of experiencing, I adjusted.

Sometimes I would get into this space where I didn't know whether my actions were coming to me or through me. Maybe you, too, have had this experience with something you enjoy. For me, I loved pruning. It can be a complex activity, a combination of art, science, and intellect to choose the right cuts. Before I even studied a book, I learned to see trees as individuals and to prune according to the structural growth habit. My choices were already coming from some other intelligence. When I worked with a tree, I lost a sense of time and felt like a part of nature, rather than separate from it. I felt my being merge with existence. I could be in this state for hours.

I continually forgot my needs. When life got crazy, the first thing that went was my personal time for myself, my meditation. I ended up doing tasks I felt were more important than myself.

Without meditation, I felt like a boat without a keel. I was drifting aimlessly, pushed here and there by the wind's will. A day without meditation became like a day without sleep. Meditation helped me to balance my external and internal life in a way that made my whole life peaceful. When I wallowed in depression or anxiety, I obsessed about things beyond my control. Retreating to my inner life created balance and was much better than checking out in all those other distractions, in order to get my mind off something.

Now, on the island, reflecting about my life, I remembered one summer at Lake Michigan. My friend and I stood on the high dunes and spotted a distant sand bar out in the lake. We thought we could swim out there and be able to stand up. We put on our snorkels and masks and set out. The lake was deep and cold.

When we got to the bar, the water was too deep. I couldn't touch the bottom. As I turned around, I was exhausted, also alone. My friend had already turned back and was far ahead of me now. My dad was asleep on a bench overlooking the water.

Panic overtook me. I was sinking, like a ship taking on water. I thought this was it. My life started to pass before me, and it felt like my destiny. Everything seemed surreal. I found myself thinking that the world was going to continue after I was gone. The leaves would rustle, everything would be the same, and my dad wouldn't even know I had died.

Then, I heard this voice: *Don't panic!* I was so startled, I immediately stopped my flailing and calmly began swimming back to shore, wondering what the hell that was. Only here, many years later, as I journaled about it, did I understand the significance.

I was sinking, but the voice from beyond the little ego self woke me up. It changed what I had identified was happening. My belief that I was drowning would have killed me. The voice from outside of myself opened me up for a better possibility.

As I said in Chapter 2, we often believe something so strongly that we're unable to see other possibilities. What is the truth? Me sinking to the bottom of the lake, or me getting back to shore?

If I hadn't heard the voice, I'd have gone down thinking it was the end, and I'd have been right! But something outside my known reality came in and saved me at that moment. I made it to shore, and I told no one.

The point is that we may think we know who we are and what is real, but there's more to us than what we can see and comprehend. Call it what you may.

Can you think of an event in your life that made you feel greater than who you thought yourself to be?

Now, during my sabbatical, I began to realize there were a lot of different kinds of meditations. I could look at a candle or campfire, watch the clouds go by, walk, cook a meal, and so on. I realized I didn't need to do it the same way every time or in the same place. A person could meditate on a park bench in public, a church, at home. I tried different places.

Did I notice anything different in the different places? I couldn't do this wrong. I learned to just sit and be still with myself. Nothing holier than that. I could be like nature, like a tree. I could let the wind and life events pass through me. I allowed space, not to create something, but just to open my mind and let the chatter go. If a feeling or event occurred, I could let it be.

I played around with what I was reading in *The Power of Now* (Tolle 2004) and my observations. By naming a flower, we make it mean something related to what we already know. We have memories of other similar flowers. We have associations with them and knowledge about them.

A second wave of understanding comes through emotion. The flower brings up something in us right here and now. We're experiencing the flower in the present.

A third way of experiencing it is with our beings, with both words and emotions silenced. This is like being a blade of grass next to the flower, experiencing it, not knowing anything but existing with it. It is, and we are. Without comparison or emotions; there is just communion with the flower. In this communion, we don't know if we are the observers or the observed. It's a still, quiet place like being in the eye of a hurricane.

Meditation can be like a hurricane. Just on the other side of chaos is the calm, like the eye wall of the ego's attempt to control everything. And when everything collapses, we can recognize who we really are.

When I applied this idea to my life, in situations with other people, my relationships took on a whole other quality. Without knowing anything about someone or feeling anything about them, I was able to see them for who they were in this moment. And they might sense something about me but usually couldn't put their finger on it.

There is no wrong way to pay attention to human nature. It's just about paying attention. It's like driving a car or weeding a garden one weed at a time. You have to keep paying attention to the circumstances, events, people, and inner inspiration so you can respond to life.

I combined meditation with journaling. I began to see how my ADD had predisposed me to see the world. It bothered me, watching my mind jump around as I sat still. For many years I thought something was wrong with me. After all, the world values people who excel at academics, can balance their accounts, debate issues, and so on. I always wanted to be like those people. I didn't acknowledge the advantages of thinking in the way I did.

In fact, I realized others who are more intellectual and logical, who had more memory and focus, had a harder time than I did experiencing the present moment. My ADD actually gave me an advantage!

I was beginning to recognize the pieces of the puzzle. I practiced meditation for hours. In one situation, I understood that I couldn't control anyone else, but I did have a choice about how I could respond to the events and other people in my life. I began to understand how I gathered information, saw the world, and what I valued as I practiced gratitude. How was I going to create a better world if I wasn't already grateful for what I had?

If you are grateful now in the present moment, that is what you get back: gratefulness. I still forget sometimes. That's okay. Adding to journal writings has helped me shift the focus from what I don't have (discontent) to what I do have (satisfaction). What I found is the universe gives me more of what I put out into it. It may seem backward, but it is the way it works in my opinion.

Your Learning Style/Personality

How do you learn best? Is it easiest to learn visually, by physically doing something, or by listening? It's important to know the learning style you're born with, because it helps you understand your limitations.

But wait! I thought I could be anything I wanted? Yes and no. The very thing that limits you is also your gift.

Would you like to apply twenty percent effort for an eighty percent return? Or an eighty percent effort for a twenty percent return? Figuring out how to align what you want to do with your natural ability will make everything easier.

How do you know what your learning style is? A lot of tests out there can help you discover this. The one I found most helpful to me was the Myers-Briggs Type Indicator (MBTI). It was simple yet profound.

The MBTI test is often used in workplaces so coworkers can understand each other's different communication styles. This can help reduce conflicts. The importance here is that everyone has a learning style, and discovering what that is is a key to discovering who you are.

Michael Meade, storyteller, mythologist, host of the *Living Myth* podcast, and founder of Mosaic Voices uses storytelling and mythology as a means of self-discovery. "The story lives in as you see yourself in it," he says. He emphasizes that we are all born with a gift, an ability to do something unlike anyone else. He calls it your genius. He suggests behind your deepest wound usually lies a gift (Meade, 2010).

Where were you wounded? What pain did you endure that made a mark on your storyline of life? Sometimes your wounds are hard to see, and because they're yours, they're so familiar, we can easily take them for granted. You may have not seen them in this light and recognized them for how they altered you for the better.

I had such difficulty focusing that I found school traumatizing. I didn't know then that I had ADD. I only knew that the harder I tried to focus, the more difficult it became. I'd started school by having to repeat first grade. Even though I valued honesty more than anything, I had to cheat to get through school. I had incredible anxiety. As my fellow students moved on, I felt horrible and couldn't understand what was wrong with me.

By the time I got to high school, I was attending one of the most highly acclaimed public schools in the country. It emphasized advanced placement and was geared toward preparing us for college. Still, I found it difficult to make sense of written material unless I was completely engaged and passionate about it. I knew I was intelligent, but I wasn't an intellectual. No one helped me to see what I could do, what was mine to do. Comparing myself to those who excelled in that environment caused a huge wound.

I struggled through college with some tutoring and graduated. But, until my sabbatical, I hadn't taken time to look at how I personally received information or looked deeper into what my learning style was. I'd been so busy trying to fit myself into the world, I'd overlooked the question of how the world came into me. I got stuck on trying "to get" what the system was trying to teach. I'd found myself, like everyone else, stuck in a school system geared toward producing a certain kind of person, suited to office or factory work, and felt shamed by my inability to be this kind of person.

I stumbled upon the MBTI again when I wanted to increase my involvement in the community of the San Juans by enrolling in a program called Leadership San Juan Islands (LSJI). Its purpose was to train local people how to understand systems thinking, how to be on local boards, and how to improve our leadership skills in the community.

It was an intense training, with thirty participants from all three major islands working closely together. Before we began, we all took the MBTI to help us understand each other's learning styles and to mitigate the inevitable conflicts that might arise.

The MBTI consists of a series of questions that help indicate a person's psychological preferences about the way they perceive the world and how they make decisions about life. The MBTI divides personalities into sixteen types.

I'm sure some of you are skeptical. How can a test prove who we are? Humans can't be categorized into parts; we consist of all these parts. Yes, you do. But everyone has preferences, and these preferences paint a picture of how you interface with the world. So, if you could suspend disbelief and try it, you might get some good insight as to what those preferences are.

Also, if you've taken a test like this before, it's worth revisiting if you're going through a major life change. In the literature it says that as we age, we tend to switch the use of the last two letters. It is said that this could be either a cause or an indication of the proverbial midlife crisis.

Though I was familiar with the MBTI and had taken a simple online version, the paid version I received from a professional trainer was much more in depth. I'd already guessed I was an INFP (see below), but I didn't realize the FP was extroverted.

My type tends to put out feelers, to scan the environment for information, from people around to the setting and circumstances. INFPs tend to take a little longer to sort through, understand, or reach firm conclusions because of gathering huge quantities of information.

It also means that, as an extroverted perceiver, listening to long conversations is exhausting. For example, one person in my LSJI cohort seemed to need to talk through everything out loud. It drove me crazy! Soon, because of our training, I learned not to blame her for her style but just to tune her out until she arrived at her point.

The MBTI looks at four traits. Each trait has two possibilities.

The first trait looks at (I) introversion or (E) extroversion. Where do you get recharged in life? Being with people or being alone?

The second looks at how you take in information. According to the test, you are either an (S) for sensing or (N) for intuition. Sensing is more focused on facts, figures, details. It tends to be practical and specific. On the other hand, people who use their intuition to gather information, are more likely to notice the big picture. They recognize how things are connected. They imagine how things could be and not just how they are. They tend to be poetic.

The third letter represents how you make decisions: thinking (T) or feeling (F). Thinkers look at all the facts then reason logically. They look for flaws in an argument. They tend to seem less personable and more levelheaded. Feelers tend to base their decisions more on what they value, and on how those decisions affect others. They tend to see the best in people and value harmony and forgiveness. They're more inclined to be warm and empathetic.

Lastly, how do you like to live your outer life? This indicator suggests that one is either a judging person (J) or a perceiving one (P). Someone who prefers judging likes to have their ducks in a row. They respect rules and guidelines, prefer to be planners, and have a clear idea what they're getting into. On the other hand, perceivers like to keep their options open. They consider rules and deadlines as negotiable. They are adventurous and spontaneous. They are fond of surprises and enjoy new places and situations.

A further refinement comes when the administrator divides the Myers-Briggs personality results in half. The first two letters are either extroverted or introverted. This suggests that your other half might be the opposite. In other words, if you're socially extroverted, for example, you might be informationally or perceptually introverted. For me, an INFP, my P was extroverted and off the charts. I scored 28 of 30 in that area. It turns out, I'm very extroverted in how I get information.

What significant score is in your type? What parts of life are you living against your nature? Where are you aligned with it?

Finally, instead of just interpreting the types and how we scored, the test administrator had each of us stand in the room representing a place where we scored, compared to others. We looked up and down the line. *Cool*, I thought. Now, this is my kind of "got it!"

Knowing your personality gives you more confidence and affects your relationships in a positive way. Whether working on teams or being in a romantic relationship, knowing each other's preferences can alleviate a lot of stress. When an extrovert learns their partner is actually an introvert who needs time alone, they can feel reassured that partner is still committed but just needs a chance to recharge.

When I was working at the tree company, I found it exhausting to communicate with staff and clients all day. This is because I was actually spending huge amounts of my energy scanning the environment (perceiving). I'd come home, and I didn't want to visit friends. Needing to recharge was a priority over seeing friends on the weekends. This was hard on me. I tried to compensate by taking a break between customers. I'd stop along the road and meditate for five or ten minutes or squeeze time in to walk in a park.

On the other hand, my horticultural work was usually done alone or one-on-one with clients. On those days, I had no trouble spending time with friends.

Are there parts of your job that stress you out? Is there a way you can alleviate it?

It helped to know I was an INFP when I took a job at the transfer station. I knew the job would suit me because it was only part-time on weekends. It would allow me plenty of time to think and study but also let me be with people. I loved working with all the volunteers. It gave me lots of chances to practice things I was learning about myself.

But it wasn't until working there that I also found out I was a kinesthetic learner. One day I was told how to operate the forklift. The person who taught me was a mechanic. His world was very logical. He thought he was giving me perfectly clear instructions. I knew that my type takes in a lot of information before we "get" it. I warned him, then explained. "You're going to wonder what's taking me so long. I take a huge amount of information in, then finally I get it, that's what INFPs do." Still, I wasn't getting it fast enough, and it irritated him. Finally, he left me alone to figure it out.

My familiar self-criticism kicked in. My anxiety rose. Then, somehow, my experience with meditation came to me. I stepped outside myself and watched myself try each lever until I found the one that lifted the forks. Soon, I was comfortable. I knew which levers to move without thinking. This was a huge breakthrough for me.

Chapter 3 Exercises

Journaling

Purchase a blank journal you feel comfortable writing in. This is your book. Choose wisely, for this is your companion on this journey of self-discovery. If you choose one and after a few sessions, you don't like it, try another. Comfort is the key here. This is for you.

Find a time of the day that you can regularly choose to write. I like the mornings. But find any time of the day that you can claim as yours.

a) What's going on in your life? Challenges? Good things? Here, write freely without editing or checking spelling. This is for you. You're free to write what you wish and about any topic! The key here is not to edit, to let the words flow. This is for your eyes only.

b) Dreams can be a great interpretation of subconscious issues. Jung would say that you are all the characters in your own dreams. Dialog in your journal about an incident, person, or event that occurred in your dreams. Ask yourself what is this trying to teach me? What part of me does this represent or make clearer? Is this something I've suppressed but might need to accept about myself? Or was this lost, stolen, or hidden away?

c) Stream-of-thought writing. Just write without stopping. Write, write, write. If you don't know what to write about, then write about that. Don't stop. How are you feeling about this practice? Try pushing ahead despite your doubts. Maybe there's a lesson here.

d) What's working or not working in your life? Follow your relativity to what wants to open in your life.

Meditation

As I mentioned, there are many books and styles of meditation. Here, I'm making a few suggestions for you to try. There are many ways to learn about yourself and about how life moves through you. There is no wrong way to meditate—as long as you're paying attention. Like moving to a new city, if you get lost, sooner or later you'll find your way. However, only if you are paying attention! So try these on and see what you find for yourself.

a) If you have a garden or a yard or know someone who wouldn't mind you pulling weeds for them, here's a practice for more mindfulness. Intention is everything. Scan the environment to see the layout of the place. There might be millions of weeds, but your job is to pull one at a time. Focus on removing one weed at a time for now. How are you feeling starting out? Set an alarm for thirty minutes. Check in with yourself to see how you are. Different space?

Annoyed? More peaceful? Feel connected? Try pulling weeds with both hands. It may be a little cumbersome at first, but give it a try. Alternate focus between hands. Then try a soft focus to see both hands moving but not the individual ones.

b) Try staring at a flame, either a fire or a candle. Watch the flame dance. Is there a pattern? What does that bring up in you? What do you notice?

c) Watch a river flow. What do you see? Leaves, insects, or branches and logs? Is it clear or murky? What wildlife visits? People? It may be challenging to try this with people around, but this is for you, not for others.

d) Sit still in an upright position. Straighten your spine and close your eyes. Because I'm accustomed to sleeping lying down, I've found that meditation works better when I'm upright, but explore for yourself. Watch your thoughts come and go. Attempt to not get attached to them. If you do get attached to them, that's okay. How do they affect your feelings? Notice a correlation? Does your mood then cause certain thoughts? Who's there?

e) Imagine taking an elevator into the earth. Create a cavern for yourself. Relax and smell the earth. Feel its dampness and silence. Feel the womb of the earth. Can you stay there regardless of the disturbances around you? How do you feel?

Myers-Briggs (MBTI)

Take the MBTI test. There is a free version online, but if you can pay for one and have a professional go over it with you, it may be more informative. Yes, the test limits you. That is the point, accepting your limitations. They are unique to you. There are patterns to human lives, whether we call them archetypes, myths, or personalities.

a) Read about your type and how it relates to you. Are you living in alignment with it? What needs to change to be in more alignment? What is the cost of not making change(s)?

b) Are you introverted or extraverted? How does that affect your relationships? Do you feel guilty taking time out for yourself, if you're introverted? If extraverted, do you get enough recharge?

c) An online source I've found helpful with the MBTI and more is Truity.com. They offer clear, easy-to-understand guidance on the types. They offer the test and things related to it. There might be a fee now. There is a blog you can subscribe to called The True You Journal blog. Your inbox won't be overwhelmed.

CHAPTER 4

What Motivates You?

Core Values

Values are ideas we believe in so deeply that we use them to guide our life decisions. Some people draw their values from religious beliefs, for example, following the Ten Commandments or following the Buddhist idea of "do no harm." Other values might involve qualities you want to put first in your life, like creativity or honesty.

Whose values are you living?

If you don't know, chances are you're living someone else's life. Our values guide our decisions. However, not everyone has a clear idea of what their values are. It's a good idea to take the time to state them so you can choose the ones you really want and then keep yourself in alignment with them. Yes, you get to choose and change them.

If you don't know what your values are, you might not know what to do when those values are challenged. What happens if honesty is important to you, but an employer or friend asks you to do something dishonest? Hopefully, you did some reputation checking about your potential employer beforehand, but even so, you might be asked to forgo your values. Are you going to comply or refuse to do what you're asked and remain honest? If beauty is important to you, are you going to want to live next to an industrial park, even though it is cheaper or closer to your job?

Besides meditating, journaling, learning cognitive functions (MBTI), following my relativity, and trying new things I'd never considered before, I wanted to revisit what values were important to me.

Some of my core values are honesty, beauty, and excellence. Thank you, INFP. These guide my day-to-day activities. When I ignore them, my inner radar goes off and I don't feel good. Our feelings are cues that something is off. Most of us can recognize when we have made a choice that bypasses our values, and we can identify and repair that choice. Sometimes it's not our actions but our perceptions that are off. We learn the difference only by making mistakes.

At the end of the chapter is a list of sample values. Please add ones not listed there that are important to you. If you have difficulty choosing which ones are most important, let your body choose for you. Put your hands in front of you. Imagine one value is in your right hand and another value is in your left hand, then close your eyes and move your hands like a scale as you weigh which one is more important to you. Close your eyes and let your body tell you.

Once you have those values, put them in order of importance as you think they are important to you now before prioritizing them. Number them one through ten. Then compare them with the Organizer, downloadable at Ericblaser.com. Your results could surprise you. As my life changed, I found some of the things I'd once valued became

WHAT MOTIVATES YOU?

less important. This might have explained why I now felt unfulfilled in my work and felt the call to something greater. I also found some discrepancies or contradictions between my different values, but once I weighed them against each other, the ones that really mattered stood out.

Does changing values help to explain why your life no longer feels satisfying? We all can change. For me, examining my values was a huge eye-opener. I could see what my old values had been and which new values I was moving toward. I gave the test to a friend who was also surprised to find that what she once thought was important didn't score high anymore.

I had moved to the island in July, and by late September, I felt restless and a little anxious. I pressured myself, wondering what I was going to do after my sabbatical. It seemed like time to find the next gig, but I was still feeling this exhaustion. I didn't want to do what I had been doing but also didn't want to start something new, without knowing what that should be. I wasn't sure how to decide. I wanted the relief of knowing where I was headed, so I could feel safe and resolved.

Over the years, I'd heard good things about Seattle Life Coach Training. I'd even had several conversations with the enrollment person. Each time, I was getting the message *no, not yet.*

Luckily, my money wasn't running out as soon as I thought it might. I was surprised by a big tax refund, a gift from my dad, and some income from other sources. I didn't have to decide yet. Life seemed to be supporting my mysterious journey, despite my own

83

anxieties and this pressure I imagined from the outside. I felt guilty about allowing myself such a long sabbatical.

I found myself doing a little garden work for an island matriarch in a wheelchair. Her garden, once beautiful, was looking neglected. The job came my way, and I did it for free. I just slowly puttered there. I didn't have to perform. I liked her, and I was enjoying getting to know the history of the island and learning more about the people I'd met at the dump.

My summer job at the dump continued into October, filling in for people who were taking vacations. I was enjoying the work. I loved that it was so different from anything I'd ever done. I loved working with the volunteers who staffed some of the shifts. Thanks to my ADD, the fast pace of work made me feel normal, and the job gave my life some structure.

Still, by November, I was beginning to slowly unravel.

As the days darkened, I got tired of living in the deep woods. The place I was renting was only about fifteen feet away from the landlord's house. I could look into their windows and vice versa, but there was already so little light, I didn't want to hang curtains. Not only was it dark, it was also cold, so close to the water. Even in July, I'd been lighting the stove to stay warm. The place was also far from my work. I was racking up thirty miles round trip a day on a small island.

I joined a Power of Now group (PON) and became friends with someone who had a winter rental available. Like a lot of locals whose winter digs turned into summer vacation rentals, I would have to move out by May of next year. It had a hot tub and much more daylight, and it was also within walking distance of a park I frequented.

Power of Now group.

I moved into the rental in early December, and we became closer friends. She, too, was going through a big transition. Finally, I had someone to really talk to who understood transitions and transformation. Before long, I found myself down at her place at least three times a week, sometimes for hours.

December darkness brought long nights, cloudy days, and almost continuous rain and windstorms. I was accustomed to keeping busy; to be living a quiet and uneventful life was a huge change for me. My anxieties grew, and I could feel, inside, things getting worse.

I continued to go to the PON group. Being a part of the conversations helped me recognize the difference between Being and Doing. I had been so busy doing, because that helped me soothe the ADD. Now, I began to recognize Being inside me, which I had experienced, but I was still unaware of. I realized the power of the present moment, which is all we have and the only place where we can change our lives. I didn't yet know how helpful this would be for what was inevitably coming.

As I considered my life and my values, I began to relate my new situation to a period I'd gone through in 2012. I'd been struggling to make money and my dream of the ideal life wasn't materializing. The stress of running a business and a household alone meant I wasn't getting my deeper needs met. My ADD was getting worse, I felt confused and insecure and kept my doubts at bay by "medicating" myself with work. All this "doing" allowed me to bypass the deeper thinking that might have helped me. Ultimately, what I thought would work didn't work.

The crisis came when several things happened at once. A close friend died, the church I belonged to divided in a major meltdown, then my physical health started to fail.

I was barely getting anywhere, and the structure I'd created didn't support me. Major mood swings tossed me from brain fog to anxiety to irritability. I found myself in a major crisis, spiritually, physically, and mentally. I wanted to run away, but I couldn't. I needed to figure out what was going on with my health, and I needed to keep my house.

Now here I was again, on Lopez Island, revisiting and even reexperiencing that dark abyss. In 2012, I thought I'd solved my problems. I'd figured out the health issue, found some more positive ways to distract myself, and kept going.

But here on Lopez, I didn't have all the work and a life in Portland to distract me from descending into the abyss.

There are those who say that before you reach enlightenment, you have to pass through your own unique feelings of hell. The events of your life conspire with what is in your own subconscious and give you the perfect opportunity to face your own "dragons," as Joseph Campbell (1973) calls them.

They say you must be willing to die before you can really live. Once you stop running and turn to face your fears, you'll be born into the bigger you.

No one can do this for you. No book, no family member can tell you what you need to know. One early mentor described this experience as feeling like the road gets narrower until there is no path. Only by continuing and forging your own path can you come to know who you are. Welcome to the Pathless Path.

Joseph Campbell describes this as slaying the dragon and obtaining the chalice. Michael Meade talks about going in the direction of your biggest fear and darkness, where you will be liberated from the little self into the bigger self.

I sat in meditation, isolated in the winter darkness. The beauty of nature tirelessly nurtured me. Where was this going?

Nobody at the dump knew what I was experiencing that winter. I couldn't tell anyone except my mentor friend in Portland. Phil understood I was going through a rite of passage. I didn't really know what was happening, and I could only trust that I would be alright.

Once again, I was afraid I was going crazy and that I'd done a stupid thing by coming to this island. In the great intensity of this experience, I became aware of the forest around me, the birds singing.

It felt like the end. Like I was going to die. I thought, *Okay, so what if I'm crazy? Come and get me! I surrender.*

If you've ever watched a nature program and seen an antelope caught by a lion, you've seen the antelope struggle to get away. Its survival depends on that struggle. But as the lion closes in on the animal, you'll see there is a point at which the antelope surrenders. It relaxes. It doesn't fight. It can't run away. I experienced this feeling of dying, of surrendering to existence. I had no context for what was occurring.

I became aware that if my life was going to end and I was surrendering to the abyss, why wasn't nature having the same experience as I was? Nature wasn't in turmoil. My internal world as I knew it was collapsing, but nature was simply carrying on. The contrast was incredible.

What kept all of life around me from imploding?

As I descended, I went from chaos to calm. It wasn't anything I thought it was going to be. Nature became omnipresent. I heard birds. I became, not a person anymore, not even an observer, but an observation. I saw from the vantage point of stillness.

It felt similar to experiences I'd had in meditation. I lost all sense of what I'd always thought was real and saw that somehow I had created both that, and now this.

Osho-Shree Rajneesh states that when you feel like it is the end, there is always more.

Although I'd understood the explanation of the difference between Doing and Being, it wasn't until I let myself surrender that I finally began to discover it for myself.

This slow building of being grew out of the dark.

One morning after my meditation, I realized that, for my whole life, I had thought I needed certain events and things to happen in order to be happy. I'd thought retirement would make me happy or that a partner would make me happy, and so on. Whatever it was, happiness was always in the future and always eluded my grasp. It was a major source of discontent and perhaps of my midlife crisis.

On that morning, I realized I could just be happy! It didn't need any conditions. I could just be happy. Because I get to. How could someone else take your happiness or give it to you? How could you ever earn it or lose it? It was a profound realization.

I began to see how I created my own reality. This didn't mean that I became free from the follies of human nature, but during this time, I learned to take more responsibility for my thoughts, actions, and beliefs.

> I could just be happy. Because I get to.

Things were so peaceful afterwards. My mind was quieter than it had ever been!

Your Passions

Passions are things you'd likely do without pay. You might daydream about it and have a sense of longing for it. If you're passionate about something, it's likely you'd get out of bed in the morning and do it right away, if you had the freedom to. If you were passionate about doing something, it's likely you wouldn't procrastinate either. You'd do it unless some conflict stopped you. It's something you'd do, if you could, even if you weren't in the greatest mood, because you'd know that doing it would make you feel better.

What are you passionate about? What activity, when you're doing it, makes you lose track of time? What would you do even if you didn't get paid for it? If you asked your friends what they thought was your gift to give, what would that be?

For years, Joseph Campbell counseled kids at Sarah Lawrence College to follow their bliss. Get a glimpse and go for it, he'd advise. Otherwise, you'll be living someone else's life.

Over the years, my happy spot had been working in gardens. I'd weeded countless hours. My guess would be that I'd weeded for over three years straight, twenty-four hours a day. That would be 26,297.5 hours. You'd think I'd have gotten tired of it, but I always loved losing myself in the activity. I lost track of time. I'd become very present and attuned to nature, as I distinguished between weeds and desirables and noticed the conditions around me. It soothed me and got me outside of myself and my troubles.

I never knew where the information came from, about what needed to get done. Information like: This plant isn't performing well here, it's planted too deep, it needs more fertilizer, and so on. The knowledge just showed up, like I'd become a receiver of a radio frequency. I'd forget that I was the doer and would become the conduit for that activity. I experienced bliss.

You may have already experienced this in your life but may not have been aware of it. What actions, when you do them, make you lose track of time? If you're not sure, see the exercises at the end of the chapter.

There is a great distinction, for me, between doing an activity and being the vessel for it. When I'm doing an activity, I'm exchanging work for money. Time for money is a prison for me. My desire to do the work is coming from the outside. I'm using the money to do or get something I want to do, later. I enjoy the idea of getting the money, and the idea of doing that other thing. But I don't enjoy the task itself. Doing a task for money can wreck the activity I even enjoy.

Instead, I've learned to enjoy the actual task. Being a vessel or conduit for what I enjoy allows me to take a big-picture approach.

The desire to do that thing is coming from the inside, from the desire to do that thing itself, not from my desire to do something else later.

You'll have to be honest with yourself. If you could do anything, what would you prefer to do? What activity makes you forget about time or lose yourself in the activity? Nobody else can tell you what this is.

One way to discover what makes you happy is just to answer the simple question. If you ask yourself "I am happiest when I'm_____," what is your answer? It could be anything. For example, you could answer: "When I'm hiking," "When I'm painting," "When I'm volunteering for Meals on Wheels," "When I'm swimming," "When I'm meditating," and so on.

If that activity allows you to expand (remember relativity?), if it makes you feel rested or peaceful and it does no harm, then you're close.

Your answers might change over time. To get a good idea of what you are passionate about, you might want to ask yourself repeatedly. Hopefully, you'll see patterns develop.

My passions have changed. I had always loved gardening and helping/coaching people to bring their ideas to life in the garden.

But after I went through my winter's passage and was able to feel what new thing I might enjoy, I decided I wanted to help other people to flower and discover themselves as they transitioned from one life to another. I want to help people cross the threshold to find clarity, find passion for that thing, and a life that works for them.

This was confirmed for me recently when I went back to Oregon to purchase some plants for a client. It was one of my last customers, a job that paid well. I'd known the nursery owner for years. She's quite a savvy businesswoman with a good sense of what works for her business. I always got good plants and good conversation when I went there.

On this recent trip back, I could see she was tired of doing the same work daily for twenty-five years or more. She confided she was ready for a change. She'd built her business from the ground up and recently built her dream home on the property of the nursery.

But I could tell she wasn't passionate anymore as a nursery owner and a successful woman entrepreneur. I'd felt the same way. Her experience mirrored what I hadn't been able to put into words.

Why not try something new? What's wrong with that?

Of course, that would mean going into an unknown zone. The resistance of the new direction. But should we keep doing the same activity while feeling this slow death of passion? Or should we face the fear of going into the unknown and the possibility of discovering some new passion?

I went from feeling like my sabbatical was a terrible idea to realizing my sabbatical was the best thing I'd ever given myself. Without it, I would never have had the time to sit still, face my fears, and rethink my passions.

The passion test helped me see the shift inside me that was trying to emerge and be expressed.

Gratefulness

The thing I learned during this journey that helped me the most was adding gratefulness to my meditations.

Gratefulness is the act of being thankful for something you appreciate that is now occurring in your life. It's something you're glad of and is the most powerful in the present moment, as something you are currently experiencing. Like the warmth of a crackling fire or a full stomach of delicious food or the good company of friends.

If you are sitting in your living room at home say, "I am grateful for my house!" Speaking this feeling allows you to put it out into the world as a positive signal of gratitude. And, since you can't have more than one feeling at a time, your life will definitely improve. Being consciously grateful for things helps me to see my world in a better light, and it's improved my overall experience of life.

For instance, I have had issues with my family for years. However, during the early part of the 2020 pandemic, we came to a big reconciliation. That was something I felt grateful for. Yes, thousands have perished and more, sadly, in nursing homes all alone. Being grateful for something that happened to me during this time doesn't mean I'm minimizing the sadness or ignoring its impact on the world. But part of my sanity and understanding relies on knowing there are also silver linings. I am choosing to acknowledge that *too*.

It's easy, especially when venturing into the unknown, to spiral into self-doubt and despair. For example, who am I to be an author? Who would want to hear what I have to say? How is my life relevant to yours? But if there's a negative aspect to something, why isn't there a positive aspect too? What if, by writing a book, I could inspire people and change lives? Shouldn't I be grateful for my desire and for the opportunity?

Gratitude primes the pump for more because you are expressing you have enough *now* to the universe. It only knows this here-and-now moment. Everything else is created by you. The absence of your desire can create discontent in the moment because it is not seen. Then you're broadcasting angst unintentionally. Similarly as when you are focusing on a problem versus a solution to a problem.

What happens to events unfolding in your life when you're in a bad mood? And the same when in a good mood? As the momentum builds either way, can you intervene? This momentum is called by some the law of attraction. That what you think about you get more of.

In a nutshell, thoughts that you keep thinking become beliefs. And then, those beliefs become your reality. Have you noticed there are so many realities out there? This is why it is good to explore you. What is good for you?

Gratitude reorients you and raises your vibration and can change your results. For example, I noticed I kept getting stuck on gravel roads and in occasional fields of clients. It took awhile to realize I needed all-season tires with better traction for rural island living.

I was pissed to spend $1,200 on them. I thought, *that's a lot* (lack). How am I going to pay for them? (lack). I was seeing what I had (reality). I was closed to opportunity.

I stopped. I instead of feeling lack and the reality of my circumstances, I bought them, then I focused on how good it felt driving on new tires, which gave me better traction and safety. "I'm so glad I have funds to do that!" "I'm so glad not to get stuck anymore!" "My next trip to Portland on a dark, rainy night will be great."

Gratitude attracts more positive opportunities into your life. You are experiencing it, so you get more.

Although I couldn't see how I was going to pay for the tires, because the reality of the repayment at the time didn't exist, I trusted beyond what I could see. Three days later, a client called and wanted help with a big project.

It took me a long time to realize how much my focus on lack has to do with my programming. How we feel has a lot to do with the programming we received from our caretakers growing up. And that negativity can suck the life out of us. But I can take responsibility for my perceptions by checking my beliefs.

Gratitude reminds us that there is abundance around. We can either make choices to support and encourage ourselves or to restrict and stifle ourselves. Which would you choose?

There is a First Peoples saying that there are two dogs. Which one are you going to feed? The one that bites you unexpectedly, growls at you, and doesn't listen? Or the one that acts like a companion, helps you hunt, and keeps you warm at night? One keeps you in fear, and the other is loving-kindness.

Practicing gratitude also helps you to face your critics. If someone says I suck as a writer, I can say, "You're absolutely right!" And it may take the wind out of their righteousness. This isn't a competition. I don't need to defend myself.

What I am saying here is there is something to be grateful for, regardless of your circumstances. It's there. If you can't see it, then ask your friends to help you. I think you'll be surprised.

Practicing gratitude also helps to get you out of the trap of focusing on the future. Thinking about something you'd like to see happen can cause a gap between what you want and what you're experiencing right now. That gap causes anxiety and stress. My experience of the nature of the universe is that our thoughts and feelings amplify what we put out, despite our intentions. To life, nature, and existence, there is only the present moment: here and now. The power lies only in the present moment. The more you focus on the future, the more anxious you become and the more likely you are to make the wrong things happen.

For example, have you ever tried to get out of debt? The focus is on debt, the universe sees debt, and you'll get more of it. The same thing goes for weight. You notice those pants don't quite fit anymore, and think, *Oh, I'm putting on weight.* Weight, weight, weight, wait. The more you focus on what you don't want, the harder you may find it to resist the things that make you put on weight. This is because you're telling your subconscious mind what you don't want, and in return it will bring you those things because you're focusing on what you don't want to be, not on doing what is healthy.

Feeling gratitude doesn't need a special ritual or a time of day. It can become integrated in your life. For instance, I remember a lunch time during the pandemic. I was feeling grateful to be working during a time when so many people were out of work and for the space around me in nature. My lunch arrived at the same time as someone else's, and I paid for both lunches. It wasn't because I wanted to get points from that person. I was just feeling grateful for my life, and that was a way to express it, simply and without strings.

Chapter 4 Exercises

Values

Here are some values. They're not listed in any particular order. How do I define them? They are fluid. Pick the ones you feel are important in your life and put them in order of what you think is the most to least important.

This is your list, not one you think would please or impress anyone else. These are yours and only for *you*. You can ask yourself: Are these values mine or society's?

No list of values can be complete, so feel free to add your own. You may also go to Eric Blaser.com to download a copy of it there and print it out.

As a reminder, you can clarify how you feel by using the following sentence: _____ is an important value to me.

Adventure	Abundance	Respect	Balance	Harmony
Family	Community	Relationships	Spirituality	Love
Peace	Creativity	Happiness	Freedom	Self-respect
Contribution	Meaning	Purpose	Beauty	Ambition
Openness	Honesty	Courage	Independence	Helpfulness
Truth	Kindness	Nurturing	Growth	Integrity
Responsibility	Positivity	Outgoingness	Discipline	Thought
Wisdom	Education	Accomplishment	Determination	Sincerity
Learning	Fun	Joy	Politeness	Change
Home	Career	Health	Pleasure	Friendship

Sometimes it is best to do this once a week for a month, or even longer, as you look for trends. Remember, shared values are important to determine whether a career or job or partner is a fit. It is arduous to try to get your employer or partner to change to meet your needs or values. It is best to know them and then choose where you fit in.

Good fun here! This is you! This is your life!

Organizer

Once you have listed your ten values in the order you think they're important to you, then prioritize them. You can find an Organizer sheet at Ericblaser.com. Compare value 1 with value 2. Choose one of them. Then compare value 1 with value 3 and choose one. And so on down the list.

Tally with a hash mark, and in the end count how many times you chose each value. Once you've compared the entire list, add up the number of times a given value was marked.

Second, compare your original list with the now-compared list. Is there a difference between what you thought was important to the compared ones?

Are they what you were expecting? Any surprises? Are some values you once thought were important now missing? Did you still have the same values from fifteen years ago?

Passions

1) Think about times or moments in your life when you were the happiest. What were you doing? What makes you lose track of time? What would you do if you didn't get paid for it?

2) Ask five friends who you trust what they think your gifts are and what you are good at. What would they see you doing?

3) Ask yourself the question: "I'm happiest when I'm_____."

4) Imagine if you had all the time and money in the world, how would spend your time? What would you do?

Gratefulness

1) Make a list of ten things you are grateful for. It could be anything, but it has to be sincere. I suggest starting a separate journal or using a section at the end of your writing journal. Once you're accustomed to this, add more. This can expand your horizons.

2) Think of something you deem to be bad. Can you see it differently? Is there a silver lining here? Add that to your list.

3) Greg McKeown says (Ferriss and McKeown 2021), that if you focus on what you have, you gain what you lack. If you focus on what you lack, you lose what you have. Reflect on what this means to you. What does this say about the nature of the universe?

PART 3

ACKNOWLEDGING THE NEXT STEP

CHAPTER 5

Nature Nurtures

Your Nature

Values, passions, gratefulness, and learning to see things in a better light are what I call the nuts and bolts of discovering who you are. Knowing more about these can help bring aspects of yourself into focus as you consider making a life change.

The next question is, how do we see the things to which we are blind?

One way we can easily gain some insights about what is going on around or within us is by looking at the environment we live in: nature.

Although your home and office are environments, what I'm talking about here are the trees, birds, and animals you share the world with, including those in your garden and in parks and other outdoor spaces. These help ground us.

The environment itself in the northern hemisphere has cycles which are reflected in our lives. The year starts out at rest, in winter, when things are hidden away and dormant. As spring arrives, light and temperatures increase, and there is a slow awakening to a roar of growth. Vegetation is able to put on massive growth only with the help of rest. Summer, with its warmth and heat, allows plants to store energy for the next season of growth by creating carbohydrates in the form of seeds, bulbs corms, wood, or tubers—food.

I bet you didn't look at it that way. We eat stored carbohydrates, either directly or by eating the animals who rely on them. Fall is letting go, where seeds and energy are dispersed, and things no longer needed slow and wither away. Then comes the return to rest again.

These cycles are a part of us, too, though we try to ignore and change them artificially. The natural world is subtle and easily overrun or forgotten. In our busy lives, connected to technology, we text our friends and family, post pictures, and push on with our business. We forget were a part of this world of cycles, only to be surprised by a life crisis: a diagnosis, a divorce, an unexpected job change, or a death.

At other moments, we find ourselves experiencing the natural world directly. We might find ourselves in a small boat at sea or away from city lights, looking up at the vast night sky or experiencing something as small as the scent of a flower. Then we're reminded of that connection and of how small we truly are.

When was the last time you sat quietly under the immense canopy of a grand old tree or peered into an unobstructed sky away from city lights? Although we don't always appreciate such passive activities, they are incredibly powerful. We're more familiar with the forceful "git er done" philosophy. But why not have another tool in the toolbox?

I recently took a trip to the Capilano Suspension Bridge in British Columbia. It's a breathtaking walk over the gorge on a bridge that swings and feels perilous. But I was astonished to see so many young people looking at the scenery through their phones! Instead of taking in the vastness directly and feeling its grandness, they were busy capturing it through and onto a small screen. If your life is constantly being reduced to a small screen, how can you feel connected to it? Where are you in the picture?

When did you last go out for a walk in the woods by yourself? When I find myself getting lost and disconnected in life, one thing I can count on to bring me back to myself is to go for a walk in nature. In some place quiet and away from distractions, I can feel surrounded by the benign, nonjudgmental peace of nature. I feel welcomed with open arms, wrapped in a breeze, submerged in greenery and open sky.

Nature is often described as a feminine mother sustaining us, offering us her support. Without her, we'd cease to exist. So why does society want to control and conquer nature? Do we know better?

Through the years, no matter what's going on, I bring my concerns to nature's feet, where I can let them go. For a long time, my life was unpredictable and often ran contrary to the seasons. But on the island in the presence of nature, I could align myself again. I could trust nature's predictability, the certainty of cause and effect. No matter what happened in my own life, I could count on the leaves still rattling, the grass still growing, all the great constants. The natural world is where I can always access and express my feelings and tears as I allow difficult childhood memories to surface. Nature is a constant strength, a place to ground and remember where I belong.

As a kid, I'd thought I was clever, burying those intense emotions then sealing them under concrete, like the failed Chernobyl reactor. Little did I know those feelings would eventually resurface and need to be dealt with.

Nature is a safe place to release our pain, voice prayers, ask forgiveness, and reframe the hurts of the past on kind ears. Nature's nature is to give. Somehow, we separated ourselves from this nurturing, giving, powerful force. Now, more often, we go against this grain. We exploit, as though we can take what we want without consequence.

A leadership program called Landmark Education (2023) talks about three kinds of knowing.

First, there is what you know. What you know comes directly from experience or from reading about someone else's firsthand experience. For example, I know how to properly prune a tree.

Second, there is what you know that you don't know. For instance, I know I don't know how to fly a plane, and without knowing how, I would know not to try it.

And last, there is what you don't know you don't know. This is perhaps the largest area in our lives. What we don't know we don't know often blindsides us, like the dreaded midlife crisis or a building feeling that something just needs to change.

Just because we don't know exactly what is going on in our lives doesn't mean we can't discover more about it. But how?

This is where nature can give us clues. The knowledge it offers can enter us through memories, intuition, or insights as we notice things about the world around us. We might notice that, in nature, a snake has to shed its skin to grow. Or that a locust must leave the darkness and shed its shell. Or that a caterpillar has to turn to mush to be reborn as a butterfly. So, what does this have to do with your life? A lot!

Nature calls us from within. We feel an urge, a pull to expand, like the galaxy from which we were formed from stardust. Nature shows us how it is possible to change, to let go of our old identities. It gives us comfort as we move into something greater.

Anyone wanting more out of life is going to encounter resistance. Fear. Our identities are going to fight to hold on to the comfort of all we've safely known, even though our greater selves want to expand.

As soon as we leave that safety of identity, the outside world closes in on us. Life circumstances get intense. We're reminded why we can't be a writer, an artist, or entrepreneur. It may be a familiar scenario or a new one altogether. Sometimes the terror is too intense, and we revert back to our old identity.

For me, going for what I want as an author, I was afraid that I might reveal to the world how worthless I really was. Then, instead of losing myself in self-confident acts of expression and allowing the greater me to flow through in a new experience, I would shut down and say, "I can't do this," and go back to my old self. Stopping myself left me feeling trapped and helpless.

What does all this have to do with nature? As I said, nature reminds us that only humans judge. Do you think the pine judges the maple? Ha, you can't hold your leaves. No. Everything just is what it is. Nature reminds us that only humans worry about the future. Does the bird worry where it will find food? No. The bird knows food will appear. The plants and animals express their true natures, which are derived partly from their genetic code and partly from their environment but also from some indescribable essence: Their experience of being alive and connected to everything else, and that includes *you.*

One way to experience this yourself is to look at sleep. You may close deals, climb mountains, create masterpieces of art, but you can't do sleep! See if you can make it happen. How does that work for you? ZZZZzzz. Fallen asleep, have you? Circumstances and events are conducive to sleep, but after that, sleep happens like grace falling upon us. So does happiness.

In the same way, nature is something we can seek out, but in some way, it has to occur to us. Let nature find you. Let it interact with you. Have a stroll in a park, a garden, or woods. How do you feel? What do you notice? What catches your eye? The beauty of the flowers? Emerging sprouts of spring? Death? Or is there an interaction with a bird or a deer that seems unusual?

Just be a witness to it. Try to stop putting words to what you see and simply observe. This may take some practice. The idea is to experience what you see firsthand rather than commenting on it. Be with the flower rather than describing it to yourself, judging, or making some kind of meaning out of it. Watch a leaf floating down the pulsing river, the sway of a forest canopy, or the clouds swirling by. What is your direct experience with it?

Do you think the trees are worried about fire? That the clouds are concerned about not being able to produce rain? Is the flower worried about fading and dying? Are they self-conscious? Nature just is. It is neutral. But it can reflect to us ourselves by what symbols we see and what interacts with us.

For example, I was driving north on I-5 ruminating about cash flow when a squirrel darted out in front of me; I braked to avoid hitting it. Never on an interstate have I seen such a critter.

It was clear this was a message, but what? I looked up the spiritual meaning, and it said it was abundance, storage, and hoarding. Hmm... I have clutter, but I'm not much of a hoarder. A few days later, I opened up my mailbox, and there were five checks!

Another example of how nature reflected to me was in great blue heron feathers. Finding them not once but three times! Once I found a long, head feather next to the writing studio. I kept it thinking, that's odd but didn't think about it further. Then, another one, a wing feather. The third blew toward me on the beach. A tail feather, and I didn't even feel a breeze. Huh, okay. Now this is weird.

A reference revealed the feathers represent the ability to navigate transitions and challenges, symbolizing spiritual awakening, self-reliance, courage, and freedom. This is what I had been doing for the past years. Can you think of something that has shown up in your life repeatedly and you ignored?

Then there are the immediate interactions like walking out in nature and observing.

On a recent walk in the woods around my house, a foot of snow was on the ground and darkness was descending. I knew an approximate direction to get back home, but there were no roads or paths. In the snow light, I could vaguely make out shapes of logs, stumps, and trees.

But as it grew darker, I started to wander in confusion. Where was I? I knew I wasn't in danger of falling off a ledge, so I didn't panic. I started to notice I was making up known symbols out of the shadows. I was recognizing things I saw, calling them steps, a garden gate, a path, and so on, even though none of those things really existed. This was interesting! I began to be aware of something about how the mind works.

In the absence of what is familiar, the mind looks for patterns and presents those to us as known or remembered symbols. This is something important to recognize, especially if we want to do something new or try again something we have failed at in the past.

The darker it got, the more my sense of panic rose. I was tripping over downed logs and was covered in snow. Just like the time when I surrendered to darkness, I surrendered to my circumstances and had no idea what to do. The sense of the Pathless Path descended upon me, and the next step to take became clear. I stopped moving and took a deep breath and stood for a moment. I looked at the trees, the snow, and the fading light. Then I just knew which way to go.

Back at my cabin, thawing out next to the fire, I reflected upon what had transpired. How again I had made it out of the situation and felt a sense of being alive, on the right path, and trusting myself.

When we feel apprehensive about making changes in our lives or embarking on a new endeavor, it helps to look at the natural world for inspiration.

Take an insect like a cicada. A cicada emerges from the ground after seventeen years. When they do, their eyes are milky. They emerge to crawl, apparently aimlessly, toward their destiny. Nature equips them with claws for climbing. Watch them as they climb. When the time is right, they start to sway. After a few moments, they begin to split their shell.

Without the resistance of the hard shell, the cicada could never properly form. I know because I mistakenly tried to help one. In an act that seems perilous, the insect leans so far out it looks sure to fall, as it lets its wings unfurl and dry. At the same time, its eyes go from milky to green to black.

Just like the cicada, we need resistance to grow. And then we need to break open that shell of our old self. Otherwise, how do we know what we're capable of? Our nature is to grow and mature over time.

But as humans, how do we deal with the fear we feel, poised between the life we know and the new one?

My first step is to acknowledge I'm scared. This is what is occurring. Second, I try to surrender to this new experience and accept it as a chance to learn. Third, I recognize that my fears may have come from some similar event in the past. Then I ask myself, how can I see this differently? Is it true I will look like a fool? If so, who cares? I challenge myself to continue anyway.

I find it fascinating that indigenous people who wondered at and respected nature were for so long called savages and treated as such. The truth is that we are the savages. It was modern man who decided to try to explain and control everything then to be angry at the rain that fell as he walked out the door. Our defiance makes us look absurd. We now think we'll go colonize Mars, but isn't that just another form of defiance?

Before I decided to come to Lopez, one of my favorite places was Wapato Access on Sauvie Island. I walked there among the fields and wild places. I could see Mount Hood and Mount Saint Helens. And when the moon rose, it was a magical place. The coyotes howled in the evening mist.

There were gigantic Oregon oaks with sprawling canopies, branches sometimes resting on the ground. I could climb up into them and sit like a bird on enormous moss-covered limbs or walk around the lake. During thirty years of visits, I watched fields become blackberry patches, then scrub trees, then cedars and firs. Experiencing the natural evolution of a place through time gave me a sense of place and a connection to something magnificently greater than me. I'd read about the succession of grasslands to forest, but to experience it was another matter. I saw majestic oaks slowly die and collapse from age and disease then decompose, whittled down by rain and billions of yellow jackets finding fiber for their nests.

I loved that place. My dream was to live on that island and farm. It didn't happen. This was part of my midlife disillusionment. But the inspiration directed me instead to Lopez, a place that has many of the attributes that drew me to Sauvie Island.

During my first winter here, I rode the ferry over in a windstorm so severe I couldn't even walk on the passenger deck without holding onto something. The crew looked nervous. The sea boomed against the hull, and spray hit the windows. Giant swells rolled by and sometimes crested. At my cabin in the woods, the wind pushed the trees to their limits, moving the crowns sometimes twenty feet. In those windy locations, their bases are swollen, mainly due to ring shot (separating growth rings) and subsequent oozing of pitch. It's their natural reaction to wind stress.

On another long walk, it started to snow. I didn't think much about it as it started to accumulate. It began to get heavy and quickly obscured the ground. To make matters worse, it grew darker. I lost track of the path. Soon, everything was covered in white, and I was lost. This time I didn't know my way, except by following the coast, which was a cliff with a sheer twenty-foot drop.

If I slipped, I would end up in the sea. Nobody would know where I was. It was like my life, all that I knew and trusted, seem to fade and get lost. Like earlier, I wanted to panic but said, "No, I can get through this."

Nature was showing me this abyss. I marched on. Soon, impenetrable thickets of Nootka roses kept me trapped between the thorns and the cliff. I had to squeeze along. After a while, the roses thinned, and I was able to head into the woods. Still no path. *Trust and pay attention*, I thought.

After an hour or so of wandering in the heavy snow, I ended up at a driveway. Which way? I had no idea. I took a left and soon knew where I was.

Back at the cabin, I felt invigorated from the walk and reminded myself of the symbolism of this journey I was on. This is the Pathless Path. The truth of surviving utter uncertainty and danger and making it. I had this deep knowing and a sense of accomplishment. I did it! I had stayed calm and trusted my instincts to let me walk along the cliff and find my way. Trust my footing. Life is about being lost at times and learning to trust.

After coming through my dark time that winter, I wasn't in such a hurry to find the next new thing. I wanted the new direction to be in alignment with who I was rather than just filling the space with a job because I couldn't handle the uncertainty. It was important for me to move forward with a sense of purpose. I wasn't sure yet if I still wanted to be in horticulture.

But it was mid-January, and I was nearing the end of my sabbatical. I had told my employer I'd let her know whether I was coming back or not. I didn't want to but was scared to cut that tie. It was known and safe. I could feel my throat and chest tighten at the thought of going back.

Despite my fear, I cut the ties anyway. Clearly, Lopez was my home. My job at the dump was extended again. Life was supporting me here, and I was getting in touch with what I wanted to do.

Between January and March, I continued to journal, meditate, and read as many books as possible. Because there were lots of retired psychologists and therapists on Lopez Island, I was fortunate that many books on psychology, personality, and child development appeared at TIOLI. I read books by Campbell, Jung, and others. Each time I had a new question, the right book seemed to show up. I had an endless supply from the universe.

As spring arrived, I felt more rested after so many years of working without days off and I felt more interested in being with people again.

I continued to go to the Power of Now and also started going to Quaker meetings. These were silent services. We just sat in each other's presence and didn't say a word. It seemed quite odd at first. What I began to appreciate was that in silence I could just feel the essence of the group and individual members. Words seem to mess things up.

It occurred to me that if people were able to shut up for a while, a lot of problems would disappear. It seemed like we were communicating in a human collective or clan. I loved to be quiet in the space. It was different, and I liked the idea of silence rather than listening to some ancient dogma or participating in a ritual that had lost its meaning through so many repetitions.

At the beginning of April, I could feel this housing anxiety again. I was going to have to move by the end of the month.

Now, I was determined to rearrange my life in alignment with my nature. To find a way of living that worked for me, my way. My job at the dump gave me a perfect laboratory to try new behaviors out. I started to practice being myself rather than people pleasing or taking all the responsibility for something not working out. I had to let go of my shame and throw away my judgments. I was always comparing myself to others, always worrying about how to deal with my ADD. I began to see how much I'd avoided anything that required me to focus in ways I found difficult.

I was also noticing how, as I practiced gratitude, I was able to see the silver lining in events I might once have characterized as all negative.

I continued to walk and be surrounded in nature, which gave me peace. I followed my passions and inspiration. I practiced finding creative ways to respond to stressful events that unfolded as a few people came at me at TIOLI with entitlement and expectations. I practiced not taking things personally. I began to learn to defuse these situations by coming out of the blue with something absurd. This seemed to throw them off and derail their expectations of how the interaction was supposed to go. Sometimes these people just froze and gave me a funny look. In the normal chaos of the job, my ADD actually helped me to stay calm and present. All the stimulation made me feel normal. But I realized the cost was exhaustion.

Was that why I did so much and stressed myself out? How should I do things? I practiced when to be firm or to say something and when to let it go. How could I be nonconfrontational and still uphold policy? How could I graciously acknowledge when I could have done something better? This wasn't easy, and I didn't always keep my cool. I was learning how to be present with people in constantly shifting situations.

Sometimes I'd feel completely out of control. I'd watch my own anxiety, then ask myself, *Do I really need to be in control? Is that the best response for the situation and people involved? Or was it my ego feeling like it needed control?* As I learned how to dance with life there, I began to be able to go with the flow or put my foot down and interrupt something that felt like it might be dangerous or not in the best interest of the dump.

Nobody really knew what I was practicing. But I got compliments from the community, and they appreciated my attitude and presence there. I loved working with the volunteers. Each had a unique viewpoint on life. One in particular, Warren, would play with me. He'd say something to me, just to see how it would land.

At first, I was annoyed. As if I hadn't taken enough already from the tourists and the annoying regulars. My seriousness was killing me. I was taking responsibility for everything and trying to control everyone's behavior.

I remember a day when a woman came in with coat hangers to donate. I said we had enough at the moment. She left and went to look around. Later, Warren and I were culling some clothes and found the coat hangers stuffed in a bag. The lady just put them there and left. I was pissed off.

Warren just laughed. "Eric, don't take it personally! It's human nature." He was right.

Warren told me many stories and taught me how to dance with life. He had a knack for saying things in a way that had five meanings to see how I would take it and where I was. He'd stare at me to see how it landed and laugh, "Come on, Eric!"

There was no way I could control Warren. Why would I? Instead, I began to play with him. Soon, I started looking forward to what I began to think of as Sunday church at the dump with him.

He was only the second person I ever met in my life who could see all the sides of any issue and not be attached to a single point of view. It was so rare! I thought if everyone could recognize that there are many valid sides to everything and that life is complex, maybe we could agree to disagree and not insist the other person was wrong. Warren helped me see that the world was more like a disco ball of many possibilities, not just simply right and wrong.

In the meantime, I loved helping people find things they were looking for and enjoyed real and honest conversations with people I was able to be dynamic, creative, spontaneous, have fun, and be my general good-natured self. And it was a job like no other—I was supporting a free economy!

As the quantity of reusable items came in, I began to be appalled at the sheer vast waste going on. And this is only one little island. (In the next section, I'll talk about how material things can't fix emotional problems.)

By now, I was down to the wire. I had only five more days until I had to move out. Tourist season was rapidly approaching, and I'd found nothing. Then, my intuition paid off again. After many dead ends, I called the land trust, just to check with them. The woman in charge said someone had just left Stonecrest Farm. There was an opening.

Stonecrest Farm was iconic, with a huge hay barn, fences, and huge wooden gates. It had been sold to the land trust and was in a transitional state, with the farmer still living in the main house. The trust had a weaving co-op and a community kitchen, and the land was currently being farmed by an assortment of local farmers. One was grazing sheep, another growing grain, and a grad student from Berkeley was studying sustainable farming and doing the local farmer's market. And there was me, figuring out my next steps.

The one-room apartment with a loft seemed out of proportion. It had a tiny kitchen and a large upstairs bedroom. It had a lovely

Stonecrest Farm corrals in the fog..

covered porch facing the common area. It was beautiful, and the best part was that I didn't have to do the farming. The mist and the sun hugging the buildings were mesmerizing. On clear days I could see the Olympic Mountains and hear the roar of the king tides from Puget Sound.

The truth was this: I was in alignment with myself. I began to recognize these feelings I'd had at times, not just in Portland, but from my college and childhood days. This is what I'd always wanted.

What is this and why were these things I'd wanted in the past showing up now?

What is latent in your life that wants to be expressed?

The first week I was there, the wind blew relentlessly. It blew all the flower petals off the fruit trees. I remembered reading accounts of pioneers going crazy from the wind. I was almost there.

After that, the summer at Stonecrest filled my soul. The full moon in the barley field, the "June-uary" mist and fog rolling in almost daily, playing hide and seek with the corrals and outbuildings. The summer was hot. I planted a squash patch, including some giant pumpkins. I'd always wanted to grow big ones for the challenge and the beauty of it. Up to that time, the biggest one I'd grown had been eighty pounds.

118

In order to grow big ones, you need the genetic potential, and you have to provide ideal conditions. You have to be in tune with the plants to understand what they need. That summer, I grew a pumpkin of 187 pounds and another of 138 pounds. That fall, I offered them to the land trust for their annual Harvest Dinner, where people guessed their weight. I got a kick out of the kids trying to pick them up and making guesses.

Still, I didn't trust where this was going and didn't know what was coming next. During a visit back to my house in Portland, I realized I needed to make a choice about the direction I was going.

It had been almost a year already. Standing on my roof with a bird's-eye view of the yard, fence, atrium, and roof, I realized they were all in good shape. I picked the mushrooms off the fence. The garage door was beginning to sag, but everything was still sound. After another year, though, they'd need replacing. The realization that I'd have to move back in for two years to avoid paying capital gains tax made me cringe.

The moment standing on the rooftop was unplanned. The thought of moving back to Portland made me realize I didn't want to. I was done. Because housing was short in Portland, too, I had to give my tenants three-months' notice. And so the process started.

Later that summer, I returned to Portland and contacted a Realtor who gave me suggestions on how to price it and get it ready. During the process of cleaning and painting, I had an urge to make it beautiful for the next person. I wanted to put love and attention into the house and landscape. My friends helped me paint, and we started to get the house ready for sale.

It's customary for Realtors to say it's the kitchen and bathrooms that matter. For years I heard this as a reason for why the landscaping budget was always cut. I didn't care about kitchens or bathrooms. Mine still had the '50s countertops and birch cupboards. But the atrium and landscaping were beautiful and lush with lots of greenhouse space.

I still had tons of hardy palms in there and around the grounds. I was concerned with how to move them out. Daily, I meditated and felt strongly, *I hope this house goes to the right person. Let the right buyer find this.*

I was sincere and put careful time into it my way. I put in an extra week and an extra $3,000. There was no going back, and it was the right decision to sell the little house that had been so perfect for me for fifteen years. My initial reason for leaving Portland was that, in the first phase of the dark abyss in 2012, I'd imagined myself here as an old man, safe and secure. That's when I realized that the reality was that, while I'd be safe and secure and everyone would see I'd made the right decisions, I'd be dead inside. That's when I'd first known that I had to leave.

What happened next blew my mind. The extra work I'd put in paid off. There were nine offers before the house even went on the market. All were well over the asking price. I had twenty-four hours to make a decision. I was stunned. The house price went into the stratosphere and catapulted the whole neighborhood into another category. Plus, the guy who bought it wanted all the palms too. What a relief! I showed him all the irrigation and drains. He told me he felt like the place was loved and well cared for, and it was exactly what he wanted.

The reason the house sold so well was that I'd ignored the advice of the Realtors who always said don't worry about the yard. So, mine was one of few places on the market that had a great yard. It set it apart from all the others. I felt I had won in the end.

A few days after I got back on the island, I saw a house for sale on Zillow. It was a waterfront property still with an outhouse and scars from a small parking area. It was basically built on bedrock. It reminded me of a house I'd lived in for a few years with my family on Lake Erie. It had a view of the water through trees. It needed an expensive septic tank, and the large picture windows were rotted. There were woodpecker holes in the siding. The deck was also badly rotten, but I didn't care. I was bitten.

I practiced focusing on seeing myself there, putting love into the place. But circumstances and events proved negative. I was already too late. The realty office said it was pending.

Up to this point, the things I was hoping for had come through every time. This time, I was disappointed. Was it a sign of a turn of events?

Material Things Can't Fix Internal Problems

Did you know that a lot of people in advertising have psychology degrees? It's because the media feeds on your psychological insecurities. If you believe you're not good enough, their advertising is going to make you feel like you could be, if only you owned this Gucci bag. Advertising feeds on inadequate self-esteem and poor self-image.

Human nature always wants the simple fix, because we don't want to get to know which deep-down core belief about ourselves needs reframing. People actually prefer to be externally focused and have a quick fix. Because inner work isn't pretty, and what do we have to show for it?

The problem with this approach is that material things only satisfy us for a short time. Then our enjoyment fades, and we're on to the next item. Maybe a new car? That's cool for a while, and we get some attention, but then the car payments are due. We end up working harder at jobs we don't like, just to make those payments. Then what? Onto the next thing, and before we know it, we're on this hamster wheel going around and around, reacting to life and not dealing with real things like what makes us honestly happy.

There is a poem included in *The Subject Tonight Is Love* by Daniel Ladinsky, translator (2003). The poem by Hafiz goes like this:

First, the fish needs to say
Something ain't right about this Camel ride... And
I'm feeling so damned thirsty

What I think Ladinsky was saying is that we have what looks like a good job, a home in a nice neighborhood, the right friends and social circle, but something is missing. A thirst which cannot be quenched.

The quest for what makes us truly happy takes time and energy. Depending on where we are and how far away we are from ourselves, it might take a few years.

Society says we have to be productive, do our duty, use our time to create something tangible. But to do something you don't like every day because you feel it's your duty might prevent you from doing something inspired, which also brings you joy.

Michael Meade made this point during a day-long retreat at an old church in Seattle. He told the story of the old lady weaving the tapestry of the world. Her teeth worn from cutting threads and her aged hands calloused, she carefully wove in the plants and animals of the earth. Being in charge of the duties of the life on this sphere, she got up and walked into the back room to stir the pot of all the seeds and nuts of all the plants in the world. When she returned, she saw that her old black dog had pulled the threads out, and the world had unraveled. She calmly picked up the threads and started to weave again with an even more beautiful worldview.

Meade talks about stories being the oldest form of communication. We're not supposed to take such ancient stories literally but use them as metaphors for our lives. For me, I was stuck when she got back and found the dog had unraveled the world. All that work, gone.

With self-exploration there, I found myself not wanting to enter the same world again after my sabbatical. If I entered the world again, I had to weave myself into it this time.

This powerful little story helped me realize I hadn't been living for myself but for other people. And I'd been seeking approval and acceptance. I'd been trying to please others and had been minimizing my desires, feelings, and needs. My well-being was on the back burner. It was gnawing at me.

This was the third time I'd been confronted with the need to take better care of myself. But this time, I saw the metaphor in this story. How many times was I going to have to hear about self-care before I did something about it?

This was a huge breakthrough. I told the group how the story had affected me; I felt a huge relief. Now I could understand why I'd been so exhausted, why I didn't want to restart my life yet, and why I had to learn how to nurture myself. I'd thought this sabbatical was just a midlife crisis. But was this really more like my soul stirring me to restructure my life completely? Was this a cosmic 2x4?

Material things are a short-term fix, but they can never fix internal issues in the long term. All around us are material indicators of success. The average wedding involves enormous expense. There are flowers, dresses, food, and so on. But how much money and time do people spend on their relationship itself? It seems to be natural to want to *show* others how well we are doing, but it doesn't reveal the internal truth.

I remembered a dear friend, years before, who worked in IT from his rural home in Washington. From his spare bedroom with fans and buzzing computers, he could reroute thousands of phones if there was an outage on the East Coast. He was great at what he did and earned a good salary and was able to buy the property where he'd grown up. He told me he wanted to make it beautiful. He confided that his parents had been abusive and addicted to drugs, and he wanted to change his memories of life on that property.

I helped him refurbish the barn and planted and landscaped it for privacy. I loved helping him to turn the place around, but I also compared myself to him. What did I have to show for all the internal work I'd been doing through the years?

The next year he got married on the property, and I provided all the flowers. As his life unfolded, he was thrown from his horse and given pain pills, to which he became addicted as his parents had been to opiates. His life spiraled out of control and ended.

I was heartbroken for my friend. But now I realized that all the work he'd done had only made his world look more beautiful. Everything he'd done externally to repair his parents' legacy and his own painful memories had done nothing to change how he thought and felt about himself internally.

Chapter 5 Exercises

Part A

This idea here is to reverse engineer your life.

What are the things most urgently missing in your life? Imagine those needs met.

Like the rest of the exercises, there is no right or wrong way to do this, no right or wrong order. This is for you and your eyes only. So let loose and see what happens! Close your eyes and imagine each immediate need met. Fulfill it in such a way that it is no longer inflamed and beating on your door, so to speak.

Invite things in. If you're having difficulty imagining, sometimes you have to invite it in by doing a mundane activity like folding laundry, walking the dog, mowing the lawn, or taking a hike in woods. Listening to music helps me.

Keep going and fulfill as many needs as you want to get to one that is key to your life now. For instance, these are mine that I did for myself as an example.

a) Financial security (imagine that need fulfilled)

b) Quality friends (imagine that need fulfilled)

c) Romantic relationship (imagine that need fulfilled)

d) Sexual exploration (imagine that need fulfilled)

e) Travel, domestic and international (imagine that need fulfilled)

f) Help people with midlife career change. Bingo!

After I fulfilled and imagined those immediate needs, I came to the thing I would most want to do as a contribution. I'd want to help people help themselves move through their midlife change, as I have in the last five years.

Only at the point when I'd imagined all my other primary needs were met, did I come to this.

If you've been surviving and struggling like I have most of my life, this can help you peer behind the curtain and imagine a life of fulfillment.

Part B

What do you want your life to look like?

Imagine an ideal life, one that really worked for you. What would it look like?

Don't worry about committing to something you might not want. You can change what you decide. Like a GPS, you have to start from somewhere before you can get where you want to go.

So write whatever comes to you, straight from the heart. Sometimes it's better not to think. If you find writing difficult, you can record it on your phone while doing some other activity.

I wrote my answers out as follows. What are yours?

1) I want to have time off to nurture friendships, cultivate a relationship, and explore myself more.

2) I want a great living and have systems in place to make things easy for me so I can support myself well and have time off.

3) I want to offer laser-focused coaching by asking powerful questions, offering support, helping people get results.

4) I want to be well rested so I can be present with clients.

5) I want to be appreciated for the work that I do.

6) I want to live part of the year in Los Angeles and part of it here in the islands.

7) I want to travel domestically and internationally and speak.

8) I want to have great health and lots of good people in my life.

9) I want to have time to relax and recharge.

10) I want to have a great support team.

11) I want a mutually supportive relationship.

These things are what would make me expand and feel satisfied. I know it's a moving target; it's going to change just like a garden does. If you're a few steps behind nature and have moments of ah... this is good! You are on. The idea you're going to love every day is false. You'll need to make constant adjustments to accommodate the endless change. Becoming comfortable with that change, instead of expecting and dreading it, is a key to happiness.

Part C

If all your needs were met and your life looked the way you wanted it to look, how would you behave? Would you procrastinate? Would you eat foods that made you feel sluggish? Would you choose to stay up half the night binge-watching TV and being tired the next day?

If you felt good, what actions would you take?

If you chose some activities that weren't supportive, did you choose them to maintain a habit? Or an accustomed familiar feeling? There are no right or wrong, just choices. How will you choose?

CHAPTER 6

Including Yourself in Your Well-Being

Become an Archeologist of Your Life

Just out of curiosity, I wanted to see what else was for sale on the island. I asked a Realtor I knew to show me a few houses, just to relieve my disappointment. Upon looking at the second house, it was exactly what I said I didn't want. A house in the woods.

Rather, three cabins in the woods. It looked like a scene out of *The Hobbit*. A 360 square-foot A-frame with high ceilings and a loft with generous windows and skylights with views of the trees and branches. It felt like a mountain retreat.

The original log cabin had been built during the back-to-the-land movement in the 1970s. And there was a small sauna/shower with skylights.

I remembered how dark and cold my first rental cabin had been, but something was different here. My body tingled. I had the feeling this was the place for at least the next two years. Something about it was calling. It felt like a great place to reflect and prepare for the next thing. This was just what I needed to feel nurtured to figure out the second half of my life.

On a subsequent visit, while conducting my due diligence before agreeing on an offer, I dug a hole to see the soil type to determine what kind of septic system I would need. I had an overwhelming sense of being checked out. Something was observing me. I stopped digging, and I could feel the trees watching me. *God, this is weird,* I thought. There was nobody around. I was in a forest.

I kept digging to about forty-two inches, and I still hadn't hit moisture. The soil was bone dry. How could these trees survive? It blew the last fifty years of my horticultural experience out of the water.

I bought the place on contract from the owner and had money left over from the sale of my house in Portland to do upgrades.

Meanwhile, back at Stonecrest Farm, I enjoyed the fading summer. Late that summer, I had this feeling I remembered from earlier in my life. At first, I couldn't put my finger on it. Then, one night in a moonlit field, out of nowhere it hit me. I was happy!

Now I had identified happiness. This was that feeling; this was how it felt.

Into the woods! On the first weekend at the cabins, it snowed. I had no heat except for the woodstove, but I had no firewood. My coworker at the dump said I could come by and get some wood he'd been stashing for his someday sauna. I couldn't believe someone would give me a truckload of wood.

That fall and winter, I started on some improvements. I experienced what I'd heard from others: It was difficult to find help on the island. People would put me off and not return calls. Eventually, I upgraded the water system and built a heated pump house and a shelter for a full-size fridge next to the cabin.

I continued to meditate and journal for hours in my free time. In early spring, I realized I needed to bring meditation and presence into my daily, ordinary life. Until this time, I'd been practicing those things separately. Now I wanted to bring it all together and integrate it. Life was calling for that. The idea felt good. But what was that going to look like? I didn't know.

I continued to practice things at my job at TIOLI. I tried to be more present and to take the community into account, the policies I was supposed to enforce, the volunteers and situations that presented themselves to me. *The Pathless Path* continued to be refined. I loved this dance.

I had so much fun and was being paid for it. People in the community came to me with words of appreciation for the job I was doing. The most support I ever had in my entire life came from those volunteers. I appreciated them, too, and all their help, and took their suggestions for improvements. I didn't feel the need to control things. I kept a curiosity about how things might continue to unfold there.

In the late summer, the Roomba hit the wall. I realized it was time to pivot. I was enjoying myself there, but I knew I wanted more. I needed to take the next step. I loved supporting the volunteers. Now I remembered the life coaching school back in Seattle. Two years before, in the early days of my gap, I'd been tempted to run to it, to avoid how I was feeling. Now it seemed like the right time to revisit that idea.

If you're taking things one step at a time, being open to existence, and trusting events and situations that feel like openings, how do you not feel like a block of wood floating on the ocean? Or a grain of sand on the beach? One cannot be in the ether and in the spirit. You're in a body, and you have bills to pay and all kinds of obligations.

The answer is: You take responsibility for yourself.

This responsibility has an amazing grounding effect on you. It can start with the things that you're not happy with, like never seeming to have enough money. Those things might be the effect of decisions you made long ago, before you were aware of what you were choosing. Until you understand these choices, it will feel like it's happening to you.

We need to upgrade ourselves, like upgrading a computer. No one else can do that for us. But we can.

What do you get out of digging up relics from your past? For me, this time spent upgrading ended up improving my relationships, refining my approach to my career and making more money, and, all the while, I was feeling better about myself and ultimately listening to the desire to write and releasing the pain of my learning disability.

The act of being an archeologist of your own life means taking responsibility for yourself and the decisions you have made.

In my many days, weeks, and months of looking into my life, I realized pleasing others to get acceptance had a cost. I'd lost touch with my authentic self and didn't develop a good sense of what I wanted. It went all the way back to infancy when I'd been neglected. My needs hadn't been met. I'd tried to be good to get the love I needed, but the effort had a great cost to me.

Maybe you, too, can remember doing good deeds in hopes of a snippet of acknowledgement from a friend or coworker or partner. Now, we all need some acknowledgement, but I'm learning chronic neglect is the most difficult kind of abuse to overcome, because at the time, we don't really know what is happening. After all, we don't have the perspective or the ability to compare our lives to others.

All I knew was that in my life something always seemed to be missing. As a child, I didn't get validation and wasn't able to negotiate for my needs. My caretakers were people who couldn't give it. My longing for love and connection was painful. I created a fantasy about relationships in an effort to manage these painful feelings.

I decided to keep myself safe by becoming independent, therefore proving to myself that I didn't need love or acceptance. Then, being so independent, I complained that I had to do everything myself.

It wasn't until I entered therapy again that I began to realize why I was there. I had a deep need for someone else to make okay my actions and desires, and I was looking for approval there too. Thank goodness, my therapist refused to give it to me. It was only when I stated to him what I was up to that he validated me. What helped was that my therapist began to listen to what I said, then mirror my words back to me. For the first time, it gave me the sense that someone was listening to me and understood how I felt. My parents didn't have the capacity or the bandwidth to nurture me.

It felt like such a relief to have someone listen, and therefore I felt important. I had flashbacks to times when I felt so alone, like I was missing something I couldn't put my finger on. I remembered a time at eight years old when I had a flat tire on my bike. Nobody was around. I felt helpless and ashamed that I didn't know what to do and didn't have the skill to fix it.

Maybe you, too, didn't get the support or nurturing you needed from your caretakers. The therapist would listen to my frustration about my mother and say something like, "It sounds like she's still having expectations of you and wants you to be a certain way."

As I began to understand the ramifications of my ADD and my needs not being met, I had an immense amount of rage, which I was able to express by beating on pillows with a tennis racket. My anxiety about leaving the oven burners on or doors open subsided. I stopped grinding my teeth at night.

Emotions have a life of their own separate from logic. Thinking about feelings created a disconnect for me. I needed to reconnect to them and experience and know them on their own.

This was why I was writing in my journal, meditating, spending time walking in nature. Looking deeply into my life was needed, and it felt good. But at some point, to really get to know myself better, I needed the presence of another—a therapist to reflect back, trusted friends, life coaches.

If you bought this book and have read this far, you are probably taking a serious look at your life. You're on the journey of self-discovery to becoming the spectacular person you really are. You are willing, like so few people today, to take responsibility for yourself, to reevaluate how you see yourself in the world, and build a new relationship with yourself that will help you make different choices and to occupy a different place in the world and level up your life.

You may have feelings of emptiness, sensitivity, self-doubt, poor self-esteem, and an unhealthy self-image. You might be discouraged about your lot in life. But digging deeper into your life will benefit you. If I can do it, so can you.

Everything came together during ten days cooped up in my cabins under thirteen inches of snow. I couldn't really get out. I had supplies, and it was COVID time. I thought it would be a perfect time to revise the book I'd been working on.

Now, the *shitty* first draft is supposed to have mistakes. Otherwise, it wouldn't get done. Writing from the right hemisphere gets the ideas down. Now the left hemisphere was supposed to make it make sense to others. For me, the first draft was written from my heart and being. As soon as I engaged my brain to make sure my spelling and grammar were good, I started to get anxious. I had these old familiar feelings of fear, failure, and trying so hard to get it right. Over a few days, it just got worse. I started to doubt my writing, my abilities, and felt the familiar fear that I was going crazy.

This time I sat with it. I decided not to react. I didn't want to go down that rabbit hole. Besides, it didn't serve me. I was trying to be kinder and more nurturing to myself now. I was trying to act differently so I'd get different results. No one was criticizing me but myself. I just sat there. The room was about 100 degrees; I was drying laundry. It felt like a sauna. Some kind of unintended sweat lodge.

I asked myself, *What is this?* I stopped writing. I just let a big gap of time pass before I thought anything about the situation. I just looked at my writing. I was mixing up sentences in paragraphs and words in sentences and letters in words. *What is going on*, I asked myself. I knew what I wanted to write, but it didn't come out right. This had been a lifelong struggle.

Out of nowhere, this voice said, *Maybe you're dyslexic.*

I felt this huge rush of energy: pain, sadness, hurt, exhaustion. I realized my brain not only had trouble with focusing, but also with mixing words, sentences, names. It wasn't my fault. All this time—fifty-six years! I wouldn't have known this if I hadn't followed my inner impulse to write. I felt so compelled to write.

I must have cried for two hours, pouring out all the years of pain and suffering. Now I knew why I'd had so much trouble with school.

What a relief! I felt renewed, lighter, more grounded. I had felt the years of struggle in school. It felt like what John Bradshaw calls the "original pain" (Bradshaw 1990) that held me back from fully embracing and accepting myself. It was the cause of my poor self-image and self-esteem I had been working to recover, bit by bit, for years.

I remembered the school I'd gone to. It had been one of the top-rated public schools in the nation. But in those days, they'd no idea about dyslexia. I'd repeated first grade and was put in special education for two more years, away from my peers. So of course, I was beside myself.

It is said that we are worthy because we exist. Period.

Repeat... Fellow human beings, you are worthy because you exist. To wrap our minds around this is gigantic. We can't do it with pure intellect.

Take a walk in nature and reflect on the truth: You are worthy because you exist!

Knowing your worth is loving yourself. When you understand what you are worth, you're less likely to overextend yourself to others, to overwork and undercharge for what you do.

I reflected on all the ways the neglect I'd suffered had impacted me, both from my parents and from my school. I'd picked up those messages and carried them as my truth. That had led to my midlife crisis. My caretakers hadn't known better and were struggling themselves.

I'd gone into horticulture because it was a substitute for human closeness. Plants are so forgiving and so flexible. Their care, as well as design aspects, didn't need much precision, and it was hands-on (feeling

Take a walk in nature and reflect on the truth: You are worthy because you exist!

and being). I'd loved the creativity, the adventure, and the chance to work with different clients. I had developed keen observation skills.

But I'd continued, for all that time, to act as if I didn't exist. Focusing on the plants and on my clients and ignoring myself. It had taken a health crisis and a sabbatical to discover how I actually saw the world, how I took in information, and so on. I'd needed time and space to learn to feel my own feelings and to remember my own life.

Throughout my whole time working in horticulture, the whispering persisted. *Write... Write...* I'd scribble things and feel incompetent.

Knowing I was dyslexic allowed me to get an editor early on and focus on the creative content and the messages I want to share. It pays to know what you're good at and work with your strengths.

Now, with this new sense of worth and the need to add myself to the equation of life, I realized I'd been giving my landscape services away in a manner that had exhausted me and hadn't honored my own needs, because I didn't feel worthy. I realized that charging more would mean working less and that I'd be more present for the clients who really valued my services.

I know that it has been over said, but it is true, that loving oneself and looking out for your financial well-being isn't selfish, it is essential. This is the single best self-care practice I know of. I ignored it. And almost like clockwork, I continued to give myself the same quality of care I originally received. Unless I became conscious of it, the neglect will continue.

Do dig. Uncover to discover.

Just like the GPS needs to know where I am before giving directions, I also have to know where I am now before I can make new choices. Particularly early on, it's hard to see the full picture. Finding a therapist or an accountability partner who is also working on understanding their own lives can really help. In moments of speaking about these things to someone else who is really listening, you might recognize patterns that are outdated, like I did. Such people can give you support as you develop new neurons (create new habits) to accommodate some new direction.

Anyone who wants real change has to practice. My accountability partner was priceless. We didn't offer each other advice but listened and offered validation.

At the end of the chapter, I'll offer more details about how to set up such a partnership for yourself.

Acceptance

After I learned all these new things about myself, what my true disposition was, what I really needed and wanted, the next step was accepting my true self.

I thought this was obvious, but in reality for me, it was difficult to do. I recognized the multitude of family, social, economic, and cultural pressures on me to be other than I was. It was up to me to graciously say no, unless of course, it was in the direction of my authentic self. I wanted to grow beyond who I presently was, and go with curiosity, graciously.

Laurance J. Peter in the famous book, *The Peter Principle* (1969), describes how people lose themselves conforming to the very hierarchy they desire in their career. This happened to me in horticulture. I was a landscape and nursery owner. I grew my business and strove to succeed, but landscaping wasn't enough. Something more wanted to come forth closer to my authentic self.

When we look to others for acceptance instead of ourselves, we give away our power to choose. For example, if I write a post on Facebook to see how many likes I get rather than it being an expression of my authentic self, I'm trading my truth for acceptance. In the long run, this can have detrimental effects on my own well-being. I can lose who I really am for acceptance from the "tribe." Impressing others becomes a preoccupation.

As I learned my values, personality, preferences, and understood my limitations. It pointed me in the direction of a fulfilled life. Once I knew those limitations, which might be different than the social ideals, I could look for the gift there. I could look for the gift! Limitation helps you see the world uniquely.

Accepting my ADD and recognizing my dyslexia and the gifts associated with those limitations let me accept where I actually was. I felt found. Now maybe my GPS could start working correctly to reroute to a life I like living.

What dark or fuzzy limitations are lurking in your life? It is okay to have them. It is up to us to accept them. If we don't, the world will show us that we don't accept them, and we will be bothered by them.

Acceptance might sound like surrender, but it's really a source of power. If anyone tries to make fun of you, you can look them in the eye and smile. You can say, "Duh, next?" If they were trying to intimidate you, your new fearlessness might even make them feel stupid.

I'm not just saying that knowing our limitations gives us an unlimited excuse. Now that I accept my own limitations, I can address them, instead of ignoring, denying, or avoiding them. I could easily say, "I have dyslexia, and therefore I can't write a book." Or, "It's a hindrance, so how can I get around it?" Instead, I tell myself it's a limitation, but I can do it anyway. I can get help.

The truth is I wanted to do it for myself. I enjoy it. I also wanted to be able to say I wrote a book! I may not do it again, but I wanted to do it for myself. Not for someone else's benefit but mine. I felt the urge and listened.

What I realized out of this whole midlife reorganization was it is best to find a vocation that is fulfilling to me, something that feeds me as I do it. This satisfaction circulates from me to others in a life-giving force. I had to bypass my old programming of it being selfish, which was awkward at first, then it was life giving.

I still get satisfaction out of horticulture. I love showing people the beauty of nature, whether it is with plants or what is possible in life.

If I had never written this book, I would never have learned I was dyslexic.

This is how the Pathless Path manifests itself.

The desire to create a life that worked for me created the path with the circumstances, events, people in my life to make it happen. I had to allow it.

And I had faith that this process of writing authentically for myself as I learned who I was might also benefit others.

But if I weren't fulfilled in the process of filling another's cup, how could I hope to serve others?

Are you serving others before yourself somewhere in your life? How does that feel?

Now that I have a better understanding of who I am, I can accept my own true nature. But it doesn't stop there.

After self-acceptance, there's acceptance of others who are different from us. Our friends and significant others, family, and others. Our ability to accept others is really a reflection of our ability to accept ourselves.

Carl Jung said our identity, sometimes called the ego, is created to deal with our original separation from our caretaker. It happens to all of us. No caretaker, no matter how young we are, can be with us twenty-four hours a day. We construct this ego self to deal with such inevitable rejection. This ego separates, categorizes, makes others wrong, and so on. It is a cause of conflict.

To give an example of learning to accept others for who they are, I visited a logging company on the mainland. They'd fixed my gas pole pruner, and the repair had failed, so I was bringing it back to try again. At that time, the state of Washington required everyone to wear masks in all confined indoor spaces. The company had a sign on the door saying *If you have a medical condition, you may not be required to wear a mask.* As I stood at the counter, I noticed that all ten workers were not wearing masks.

Thoughts ran in my head. I imagined their political views and their lives and compared them to mine. Trump supporters, anti this and that. They maybe were people I wouldn't want to associate with, and so on. I saw them looking at me out of the corners of their eyes, perhaps judging me as I was judging them.

They knew I lived on an island and had a long journey to return for the repair, so they took my pole pruner and proceeded to fix it on the spot. Apparently, water in the gas again. They replaced the carburetor a second time and added a gas cap for free, thinking perhaps it was letting water in. No charge.

I felt taken care of. They'd gone above and beyond to make the situation right, even though it might not have been their fault. At that point, it didn't matter what they believed. What mattered was how they'd treated me. By the time I left, I'd accepted them as they were, period.

Acceptance can change your life. As you accept, it dissolves differences. As you accept those parts of yourself that have been rejected, peace naturally takes its place. As you accept your true nature, joy flows. As you accept, then the right action can come naturally. For me, it was returning to that shop again, because they took care of me.

What Nurtures You

Earlier in the book I mentioned how my relativity and opening and closing to what felt good became my guide. Now, what activities, what kind of people and places make you feel energized?

First, I had to identify what was nurturing to me. What does it feel like, and when do I feel it?

It can come from a coworker who acknowledges how hard I worked to get my part of the project done. It could be flowers from a neighbor or a holiday spent with family or friends. It might be the act of creating a meal together with people you care about or having time to yourself, without the daily grind of obligations. It could be a simple as sitting under the night sky alone admiring the stars.

The important thing is to begin to look for that familiar feeling where you can acknowledge, "Yes, this feels good. I need more of this."

The feeling can be as simple as the act of coming out of the rain and warming up by a fire. It can come in contrast to some discomfort. I was first cold and hungry, and now I'm warm with hot cocoa.

The feeling of being nurtured can come up unexpectedly. I could go to a party not knowing anyone but suddenly feel like I belong. It's the good feeling I get after an interesting interaction or after visiting some place that inspires me.

Contrary to nurturing, I ask myself, what does doing something out of obligation feel like? What's going on that makes me feel driven to go out of my way to help someone, even though I don't want to? Can I slow that down and be honest with myself?

For about fifteen years, my dad had been out of my life. Suddenly, he wanted to reconnect. At first, I was suspicious. I thought he must be dying or something. We started on Facebook with a "Hi" and then progressed.

When he first left us, I'd been stunned. I'd broken a few tennis rackets in my rage. How could he leave? He'd been gone for most of my childhood anyway. After the rage came my struggle to become independent, to give myself the love and nurturing I felt I'd missed. Eventually, I'd come to forgive my father for what he couldn't give me.

He'd never visited me during the years I'd lived in Portland. By the time he reached out to me, I was over it. I'd moved on emotionally. Of course, I still felt the wounds, but they had less power, because I'd become conscious of so much. I'd let go of my intense feelings.

Two weeks before leaving on my sabbatical, he'd called and said he wanted to see me in Portland. I told him what I was doing. He'd insisted. I'd told him I might not be very present, but if he really wanted to see me, then come.

I was being honest about my situation and open to his visit. Somehow, we ended up on a park bench in downtown Hood River.

My dad said, "Son, you look really good."

I paused for a while. Here was my opportunity to express how I really felt, honestly without blaming him. I said, "Dad, I have spent tens of thousands of dollars on therapy to get over my childhood. It has been really hard. I'm finally in a pretty good place."

My dad said, as people passed on the busy sidewalk, "I know, son. I was a jackass."

I couldn't believe what I'd just heard. I hadn't blamed him or caused him to get defensive and resistant. I'd just stated my truth, and he'd validated it simply and wholly. It was one of the most satisfying experiences of my life with him.

The whole scene felt like a movie almost twenty years in the making. I never thought I'd have this opportunity, and I didn't know if I'd have more time with him beyond this point.

In the following years I dug up old memories and processed our relationship, and more and more of the old feelings lost their "charge." I cautiously extended myself to him.

We began to talk weekly. It didn't feel like an obligation. We talked about what was going on in our lives, both now and then.

I asked him what it had been like to raise us kids. He confessed that he'd often had to visit a loan shark to get a loan to make it to the end of the month. When he said that, the pain I'd carried for all these years about asking for things and getting shamed and rejected for it seemed to vaporize. Now, we were able to nurture each other.

I asked him how he dealt with doubting himself as a musician, playing in the Cleveland Orchestra, shows, and so on.

He said, "You can't let it bother you."

I asked him, "Does it ever go away?"

"No," he continued. "You just have to learn how to deal with it."

Priceless. From my father, fellow artist and sensitive man.

It soon became one of my best nurturing relationships. My dad got a do-over, and I got the dad I never had.

Chapter 6 Exercises

a) Accountability partner. Find someone you have an affinity for, who is also in recovery or on some authentic path in life and would like to join you in your effort to change. This can be someone in your community or somewhere else. As long as you can talk to one another.

1) The topic is what's working and not working in your life. Anything is open for discussion.

2) Nobody is in charge. Take turns sharing and listening. As you listen to the other person's story, stay grounded and present in what they're saying. Don't think about how you should respond. Be careful especially not to judge, project, or offer advice unless they specifically ask for it. No one wants to be told what to do. Instead, try to repeat back to them what you heard. It might not be something they're conscious of, but they might hear if you summarize what they seem to be saying.

3) When it's your turn, listen carefully to their feedback.

b) What activity are you doing that is outdated and no longer serving you? Why do you do it? Is it out of habit, obligation, or a stepping stone? And if it's the latter, is there another way?

c) What inside is calling you to the surface? Do you want
    to start your own business, take on a leadership role
    for the company you work for, take singing lessons, or
    something else? What calls you to expand and reach
    for something greater?

    What is in the way? What comes up? What happens if
you acknowledge your resistance and do it anyway?

CHAPTER 7

Full Circle

Aspects of Ceremony

Everything has a beginning, middle, and an end. By now, I've reflected on my life and my nature; I have a better sense of my story, how events shaped me, how I changed. I have taken the important space and time alone to be present in my life and to discern what is from what was.

When I went back again to Portland at my four-year mark on the island, it was clear I wasn't the same person who had left.

I went past my old house, visited a grocery store now converted to an Asian supermarket. I walked down through the Hawthorne District seeing lots of changes. I was flooded with memories of experiences that had shaped me into the person I'd become.

I passed a low stone wall where twenty-five years ago I saw a man pressing polished stones into fresh mortar. I remembered him so clearly. Now the wall was covered in moss and duff. I remembered who I'd been, all those years ago. Portland had changed, and I had changed. The past is in the past, and it was important to acknowledge that and to let it go.

Wall with accumulated duff.

What aspects of your life are you experiencing that are now different? What places could help give you a sense of the passage of time in your life? What were you doing and struggling with? What has passed?

How can we change if we're doing the same old activities?

This is why creating a ceremony to acknowledge those changes is so important. Most people don't have enough time to eat, let alone the time to acknowledge their passage from phase to phase in the course of their lives.

But if we ignore these changes, we can get stuck repeating ourselves. It's like trying to rekindle your relationship by going back to the same restaurant you went to on your first date. You can't move forward by going backward. It doesn't work.

I also tend to want to forget the negative experiences instead of consciously letting them go. Sadness, fear, and pain are unavoidable, but if I ignore difficult events, they can continue to influence me without my awareness. Even if I didn't have the capacity to acknowledge them at the time or have managed to forget about them, they reside in me and cloud my present-day experiences. Avoidance keeps events alive. But to recognize, acknowledge, and respect them allows us to move on. Moving on makes me ready for the next experience and makes me more present and alive.

My accountability partner had spent some time in a convent. She began to explain to me what she'd learned there about ceremony. She had learned to think of her passage in three phases. Recognize, acknowledge, and receive.

The first is to *recognize*. I recognize that something has shifted. Something at work, in my relationships, or at my core. There's a stirring inside of who I was and now who I am. This can be subtle. Like a soft, warm breeze or a scent from a far-off rose. This is relevant to you and only you.

The second is to *acknowledge* this by taking it all in and feeling it—the good, the bad, and the fuzzy. What have I learned? I just sit with the messages I get. Perhaps I've increased my skills, developed connections, gained some deeper awareness of who I am.

The third is *respect* it. What is the wisdom of the situation, the lesson my job (marriage and so on) has taught me that I can now be grateful for?

Ceremony helps us move through the story of our lives and can ignite a fresh urgency to manifest our new purpose. Who have you become? What's next?

Meanwhile, back on Lopez, it's hard to believe another year has passed. If I could have seen who I'd become, I'd hardly have recognized myself. My friends in Portland now comment how happy I look.

Thank goodness I was open to exploring and was willing to let life fall apart. And it did. But to my surprise, there was another life beyond the one I thought I had. And, existence had my back, created situations and events that helped me move forward, and supported me with a job and a place to live and with surprising checks in the mail.

Then, my thoughts and feelings crystallized into focus. I learned I'm good at nurturing plants. I left myself out of self-care, and that led to burnout. The process of changing my old patterns felt so awkward and intense. The guilt! It felt so strange to say no and to stop accommodating everyone. I made myself take Sundays off, then expanded that to two days. Not working at the transfer station felt painful at first, but taking time to rest soon turned into more energy and allowed for more income. After a while, nurturing myself better, I felt my desire to care for plants slowly return, along with a new sense of worth and value.

As I reflect back on my work in horticulture, I *recognize* my soul wants more out of life. It wants to grow. Things aren't the same anymore, and it is time to expand.

I *acknowledge* horticulture has been a place of solace and refuge and self-learning. It gave me interest, passion, and sustenance.

I *respect* it. I've done horticulture as an artist. I have an eye for beauty, pruning, and plant design. I approached it as a craftsman. I am satisfied with my approach and with what I achieved.

As soon as I acknowledged all that, people started showing up asking me to teach them about horticulture. Not just the surface knowledge, but its spiritual connotation I have described here. It was the perfect answer, and because I could feel the need for a shift and was present to it, it began to happen.

One of my clients was a single mother who had a child with significant challenges. I began to work with him, planting things, and soon became an adult figure in his life. In addition, a colleague recognized my keen pruning abilities and asked me to teach him.

Looking At the Story of Your Life

We looked at ceremony as a way to recognize parts of our life that seem to be ending or needed to end. Now we are going to connect these endings into the natural beginnings and string the narrative together to have a look. The final progression after recognizing the need to let things go is to look at the record of your life.

In my life when something is falling away, something new is always coming into view even if I can't see it. These passages of events in my life are my story. We create a narrative that connects events in our lives to make meanings. This is either unconscious or conscious. We humans are meaning-making machines. You are making your own story.

For me, the new thing that showed up was mentoring. Not only teaching others about horticulture, but also being there for the growing number of people who feel comfortable talking to me about deeply personal things.

This also seemed to come out of the blue. However, becoming a coach for people moving through midlife feels right on my path, the next step. I don't have to go out of my way. I cross the line continuing the path and trust.

How did I find this path? I listened.

By now, I have a certificate from a coaching school, and I've written a book about midlife crisis. Both are bold moves, far beyond who I once saw myself as being.

Now you have also hopefully started to recognize yourself in your own story, have experienced synchronicities, and can feel your next moves.

The purpose of including my own life events here has been twofold. First, perhaps you can see how my life worked out even though I didn't know what would happen. Second, this narrative helped give real-life examples applied to what I was talking about. The logical aspects were bricks and the narrative was mortar, hopefully inspiring you to live your own adventure.

It is worth repeating here that the idea is to cocreate your story with existence and not to wholly generate it from your "knowing." The left brain likes to figure out what to do in advance, laying out a logical sequence of events. The right brain likes to let the story unfold.

When I speak of story here, I mean big story. I don't mean the story I tell myself to justify who I am because of how awful people have been in my life, how bad my client is, how I can't go forward in my life because of something that is preventing me, like my dyslexia. These things are likely the little self's brain telling us to stay the same, stay safe. I'm talking about that thread of your life that you get glimpses of at times. Those aha moments. My spirit was calling me to grow.

The best way to explain this is by summarizing my own story again, as an example.

I left the tree company because I took responsibility for recognizing that their values and service model didn't fit who I was. I took a sabbatical to figure out what I really needed at this point in my life. I'd been in love with plants. The more I nurtured them, the more they gave back to me. But I'd lost that feeling. I needed to grow again. I left the world I knew.

After reviewing my life and letting it unfold in a new way, I realized I could use my gardening skills as a metaphor to help others understand their lives rather than throwing it out. I learned valuable lessons through gardening. If the nature of the universe is to expand, and we are made like the earth out of the same materials in the same proportions, then our nature, too, is to expand. How can we be different?

Back in college, my first idea of myself was to become a stockbroker. After my impoverished childhood, all I wanted was to make money. I'd been working at a brokerage firm when I had a series of mystical experiences that completely changed my life.

I had a series of out-of-body experiences and premonitions. It was so out of left field. I began reading New Age books to try to understand what happened to me. That's when I first became fascinated with life, its meaning, and purpose.

Now I see that since that time, I'd been leading two lives. One became a mild-mannered horticulturist trying to forget a troubled childhood. The other, lurking underneath, was a spiritual seeker wanting to understand the nature of reality. That version of myself had always been interested in philosophy and in reading and writing. It took years before I ended up on this island, reconciling my experiences and my impulses, before I realized where this urge to write was coming from.

Back in Portland, I'd tried to write a screenplay, but I'd found it so difficult to focus that it took hours just to write a page. Through the years, I kept trying and enjoyed it, but eventually it was so slow and frustrating that I remember, after buying my house, sitting at my favorite coffee shop in Portland thinking I'd better get serious about landscaping and make some real money. There, I let go of my desire to write.

Fortunately, on Lopez, writing had come back. I first wrote in journals, listening to the whispers within. Then I recognized how hard it was to find a good book about what I was experiencing. I wanted to share my experiences and coach people through this confusing time so they wouldn't feel as lost as I did.

Piece by piece, the Pathless Path appeared. Eventually, I realized I am a creator-innovator type of person. I didn't really talk about my mystical experiences with many people. My spiritual nature was opened early; however, it now wanted to be integrated.

I made the bold decision to get into a book writing program. I wanted to complete the book. I didn't know I'd find out I was dyslexic. When that happened, I thought, *If nothing comes of this writing, then just finding that out was worth it. I have nothing to lose. It is who I am, now.*

For most people, it's hard enough to write. But it's even harder to write with no idea where you're going. Then there was the ADD, which made it even harder to focus. I had to learn ways to be with that and not let it create more anxiety by reviving that old sense of worthlessness, the sense that there was something wrong with me.

Toward the end, as I was practicing nurturing myself, I realized I needed more editing help. I found an editor on the island and sat at her table in complete frustration, close to tears, telling her my story and my problem. After listening to me for over an hour, she said, so unceremoniously, "Eric, you're an artist." Somehow, I heard it this time. It hit home as truth.

I write because deep inside, my being is crying out to Write!

But that didn't mean I had to do it all myself. After that, I'd just do the best I could, then let my editor rearrange it while I kept working. It was another act of self-care, like mandatory days off so I didn't have to struggle so much.

I write this because it is my story and because of all the connections that have led me here. And, specifically, because I couldn't find a good midlife-crisis book relatable to me.

What past experiences are you reminded of as you embark on the second half of life? Who were you once? The creative person who got suppressed, who might now be resurfacing with fresh enthusiasm and talent?

Making Changes

Now that I have made new connections that make sense to my life and story, what appears to be my next move?

If the answer isn't glaring at me, then I'd better wait for inspiration. If you followed me this far, you should know this. Put the doer aside, the pusher of the river, and stop demanding.

Relax and wait. Perhaps put a little tension on it, to activate the universe to help. I could tell myself, "I'm ready to know the next step of my life." I'll know; my relativity will confirm it. Sometimes the things that come won't make sense.

By now, I started to recognize a few common threads and themes. Sometimes I just have to get moving and try something then make the appropriate adjustments if it isn't in alignment with who I am. I'm not worried. I can pivot.

My guidance had already told me to move to another state. On an island. I wasn't expecting that step; that guidance was scary as hell.

Big changes might feel fake in the beginning or cause us to doubt ourselves. But, may I suggest, as in the earlier chapters, just to play at this new thing. Just to see what happens.

Being curious changes everything.

The pressure to leave my job at TIOLI at the transfer station was building. Still, after learning and practicing the essential need for change and growth, I just couldn't hit *send*.

I knew it was time to leave the job I'd learned so much from. I'd sat in my truck thinking, *I have to send this email to the district manager. I'll do it later. When I get home.* Then it would be after I ate. I kept on putting it off, making excuses. Something was up. Was I afraid of losing a chunk of my income? Or that I wouldn't see the people I still enjoyed working with? Would I feel more isolated?

I'd come here, after all, to figure out a life that worked for me. I wanted to have integrity and to be authentic to who I was. How did I find myself once more in a position where, like the tree company, I was coming home exhausted? Not so much because of the physical work but from all the communication, problem-solving, and public contact.

When I first arrived, I loved how simple yet profound the system was. You had two choices: Take it or leave it. I can't tell you how many times I used that line. In countless other scenarios, I'd just say, "Take it or leave it."

How different it was from anything I'd ever done. Shoplifting? More like stealth drop off. We'd have to be on the lookout for things no one would ever want to take. An old coffee pot with a cracked carafe. "It's still good!" Then why are you dropping it off?

It was time to quit, but I kept dragging my feet. Why? Once again because there was no clear path beyond hitting send.

I imagined myself done with the job. Feeling the relief of having my weekends back without all that intensity. It felt good. I knew this was the right move. I sent the email.

Out of the blue, a new gardening client came.

Still, I was concerned about the winter. I'd spent my extra income on a writing coach and didn't have my normal winter funds. I was sitting in my truck when I got a call from a former client who needed help. A fire had swept through his RV park in Estacada, Oregon. I'd worked with them for almost twenty years. They needed a replant.

How do you know it's time to leave a job, place, or relationship? Simple, when it no longer serves you.

A good metaphor is to imagine each phase of life like a canoe. A canoe can help me cross a lake. It keeps me safe and dry until I get to the other side. But to hold on to it and carry it beyond its use on the water is a struggle. What if I come across another body of water? What if? What if? Then what is really the concern here? Fear. Fear of the unknown, fear of the unknowable. The truth is, I can't control every circumstance, but I can control how I respond.

The TIOLI job was a gift when I needed it. It helped me grow and practice what I was learning. But it was a canoe, and when I left it on the new shore, the next phase of my journey unfolded. It became apparent that I was on the other side of the lake and needed to move on to get more into alignment with who I had become.

This alignment, if you ever felt it, is like being in sync with a dance partner, feeling a song that moves you and stimulates your inner being. Or, it's like the feeling you get from seeing the night sky away from city lights. I'm sure everyone has experienced alignment but may not be conscious of it.

I had to go on sabbatical. Back in Portland, I had friends, comfort, predictability, and safety. I had to leave this world behind to go into the unknown alone and take the Pathless Path. It took a long time to learn how to trust myself, and I wish I had this book as my companion along the way.

Chapter 7 Exercises

a) What areas of your life have changed? How could using the aspects of ceremony benefit you? And after completing an example of change, does your life feel richer?

b) Connect events of your life into a story. What meaning are you going to give it?

c) Where are you now in this story? How are you different? What is the next step for you?

CONCLUSION

In the End

I started this journey by making a commitment to find a life that worked for me. Once I did that, the universe lined up and the Pathless Path opened and showed me the next inspired step. Hopefully, this book was one of those inspired actions that helped you on your journey.

As I stated, there was much introspection, revisiting my life, connecting to my ongoing story, personality, values, and abilities. It was a success. It didn't always feel that way, and I often wondered what the hell I was doing. This is likely going to happen to you too. It is a part of the process of discovering who you are in the next chapter of life.

Please try to remember to be kind to yourself. I spent months at a time being critical and doubting myself, afraid to share the very book you're reading. Once I realized the block to self-expression was rooted in how I received care and nurturing and what I made up about it, (nobody listens to me, I'm not important, and so on), I sought help from a coach to put it into perspective and let it go.

Other times I got caught up with life and put everything on hold, dealing with upgrading the infrastructure at my home, or my work got busy. At times, I got so involved with writing, reading, and working on myself that I forgot about making money until I was out of it. It is difficult to balance life, work, self-exploration, and learn a new career. This is all a part of the journey too! The contrast enhances you. It is an incredible act of self-love to take responsibility for your life. Keep going!

I was doing horticulture all along and simultaneously writing and exploring what this next chapter would look like. The book writing tied everything together for me. What could do that for you? Follow your inspiration.

The ultimate gift I learned out of reevaluating life is to realign or align for the first time to a livelihood that feeds you while you do it. It is life-giving for both you and those you serve. You don't get exhausted but energized.

> # A livelihood that feeds you while you do it.

That activity is usually something you take for granted, like the kid in the introduction who liked to edit skateboard videos. It is hard to recognize because it is already your nature. Others can help you identify it.

For me, whether writing, gardening, pruning, or coaching, it is bringing and enhancing the divine beauty of the natural world into people's lives. I love it. It is my nature. It feeds me.

What activity feeds you?

People close to me saw me as an artist, but I couldn't see it. More honestly, I didn't want to accept it. It scared the shit out of me. I already had limitations because of my learning disabilities and had spent most of my life trying to be like those who excelled at more worldly and practical things. I didn't have the support I needed to understand.

I didn't want to accept *artist* to the mix. I didn't want to deal with another thing to cause me strife. For the world mostly doesn't look kindly on artists. It can be a hard way to make a living.

Only after accepting my artistic nature did I finally see my father as an artist. I remember thinking I didn't want to be like him. Thank goodness I was able to reconcile our relationship and acknowledge him for it. It isn't easy to do. I know.

But in the end, I learned I can't live fully unless I accept myself and consciously choose rather than react. I am much better at that now. I'm still improving. The freedom it brings is amazing. It feels like I am now whole. Head and heart connected.

I hope this book has helped you recognize this in yourself. Your life is your own journey. It begins with so much uncertainty. There were so many times when I wished for something to guide me on my way, to help me trust my experiences. I hope this book helped you trust your experiences as you head into the unknown, down into an abyss of reidentification. You'll be okay. Trust the process. I made it. You can too.

Enjoy the journey!

If this book helped you gain clarity in understanding the story of your life, please leave a review at your favorite online retailer so this book can reach the audience it was intended.

CONTACT THE AUTHOR

Eric A. Blaser
34 Military Road
Lopez Island, Washington 98261

www.ericblaser.com

Cell phone: 503-939-8444

IN GRATITUDE

There were many people who were instrumental in helping me get this book done, either directly or indirectly. I'm so grateful. Not all of them are listed here.

First and foremost, the Get Your Book Done Accelerator Program with its coaching and writing modules has been priceless. Karen Fisher, whose brilliant guidance and editing rearranged my words for clarity and saw me for who I was, an artist. Kim Norton, who carefully read the manuscript and gave sound advice. Ted LaBrue who helped bring more clarity in the end to the manuscript.

Phil Valette, "Pathfinder Agate Man," whose wisdom of rites of passage and transitions leaned his ear to help me understand what I was going through. Jeffery Berger, who was a great sounding board and offered therapeutic advice. Sandy Levey-Lund, whose On Purpose coaching helped me move through fears of self-expression. Jenny G. McGlothern, who encouraged and supported me on the journey of self-care.

Joseph Koutney, whose hand in friendship and hospitality helped smooth out the transition to the island. The Lopez Island Community, whose warm welcome helped me feel at home. "The Dump," which provided the place to practice the Pathless Path. Warren Hero, whose clever wit and wisdom played with me at TIOLI. Nijen, who clued me on to the magic of the present moment. Silvia Ferreira's laser-like awareness kicked my ass and wizened me up. Kate Scott, living her beautiful artistic self.

My father, with his steadfast support and friendship. Crystal Springs Rhododendron Garden in Portland, which has offered solace, reflection, and beauty for over thirty years. Andy and Andrew Robin, who offered reading feedback. Finally, Pedro, who held my hand on the beach.

REFERENCES

Bradshaw, John, 1990. *Homecoming: Reclaiming and Championing Your Inner Child*. Bantam Books.

Cameron, Julia. (1992) 2002. *The Artist Way; A Spiritual Path to Higher Creativity.* New York: Jeremy P. Tarcher/Putnam.

Campbell, Joseph. 1973. *The Hero with a Thousand Faces.* New Jersey: Princeton University Press

Dictionary.com. 2020. "Relativity." https://www.dictionary.com/browse/relativity.

Eisenstein, Charles. 2021. "The Revolution of Reunion with Charles Eisenstein." The Aubrey Marcus Podcast, December 8, 2021. https://apple.co/2lMZRCn, https://spoti.fi/2EaELZO

Ferriss, Tim and McKeown, Greg. 2021. "#510: Greg McKeown—The Art of Effortless Results, How to take the Lighter Path, Joys of Simplicity, and More" in *The Tim Ferriss Show.* Podcast. https://open.spotify.com/episode/2Aoo8KvMyWwPeOYkvQxelY

Frost, Robert. (1915) 2015. *Road Not Taken and Other Poems.* New York: Penguin Classics.

Ladinsky, Daniel. 2003. *The Subject Tonight is Love: 60 Wild and Sweet Poems of Hafiz*. Penguin Compass.

Landmark Education. 2023. landmarkworldwide.com

Luna, Elle. 2015. *The Crossroads of Should and Must: Find and Follow Your Passion*. New York: Workman Publishing Company.

Meade, Michael. 2010. *Fate and Destiny*. Housatonic, Mass.: Greenfire Press.

Moyers, Bill. 2011. *Joseph Campbell: The Power of Myth*. Knopf Doubleday Publishing Group.

Murray, W.H. 1951. *Scottish Himalayan Expedition*. London: J. M. Dent.

Peter, L. J., Hull, R. 1969. *The Peter Principle: Why Things Always Go Wrong*. New York: Morrow & Co.

Rajneesh, Bhagwan Shree. (1987) *Beyond Enlightenment*. Boulder, Colo.: Childress Foundation Inc.

Solomon, Takaya Patrick, dir. 2011. *Finding Joe*. Produced by Churchill, Frazer, Solomon Gaia. Amazon Prime.

Tolle, Eckhart. 2004. *The Power of Now: A Guide To Spiritual Enlightenment*. Vancouver, British Columbia: Namaste Publishing.

RESOURCES

Material that influenced me to self-discovery:

Atwood, Janet, A and Chris. 2008. *The Passion Test.* New York: Penguin Group.

Bridges, William. 1980. *Transitions: Making Sense of Life's Changes.* New York: Addison-Wesley.

ABOUT THE AUTHOR

Eric A. Blaser left Portland, Oregon, on a six-month sabbatical to discover who he wanted to be in the next chapter of life.

Armed with a violin, screenplay, and an old boat, nothing went as planned. But everything unfolded perfectly in the process of uncovering the past and rediscovering his nature. He reconnected to his lost artistic and spiritual self and continues his storyline of life.

Eric currently lives in the San Juans of Washington State with his black cat, Edwene.